KITCHEN MAGIC

Commissioning Editor: Lucy Carroll
Design and Art Direction: James Empringham
Production Controller: Marion Storz
Food styling: Becks Wilkinson
Prop styling: Lydia Brun

Published in 2025 by OH
An Imprint of HEADLINE PUBLISHING GROUP LIMITED

1

Cataloguing in Publication Data is available from the British Library

ISBN 978-1-0354-2965-3
eBook 978-1-0354-2964-6

Printed and bound in China

Headline's policy is to use papers that are natural, renewable and recyclable products and made from wood grown in well-managed forests and other controlled sources. The logging and manufacturing processes are expected to conform to the environmental regulations of the country of origin.

HEADLINE PUBLISHING GROUP LIMITED
An Hachette UK Company
Carmelite House
50 Victoria Embankment
London EC4Y 0DZ

The authorised representative in the EEA is Hachette Ireland, 8 Castlecourt Centre, Dublin 15,
D15 XTP3, Ireland (email: info@hbgi.ie)

www.headline.co.uk
www.hachette.co.uk

This book is a reference book about the history of cookery and plants in Witchcraft. This book is not intended as a replacement for professional medical treatment and should not be relied upon as recommending, encouraging or promoting any specific diet or practice. It is also not intended as a guide to which plants/ingredients are edible or have nutritional or medicinal benefits or to replace the advice of a nutritionist, physician or medical practitioner.

We strongly advise you to consult a medical practitioner before using any herbal remedies, especially if you have an existing medical condition, are taking medication, are pregnant or are breast-feeding. You should not use the information in this book as a substitute for diagnosis, medication or other treatment prescribed by your medical practitioner.

There is the possibility of allergic or other adverse reactions from the use of any plants mentioned (and plants not mentioned) in this book. You should seek the advice of your doctor or other qualified health provider with any questions you may have, especially in relation to medical conditions or allergies. Some plants may interact with prescription drugs including, but not limited to, the Pill and anti-depressants; if you are using any medication you should always consult with a qualified medial practitioner before taking any herbal remedies.

The publishers and author do not accept any liability for any harm that results from your use, or misuse, of this book, or for your failure to seek appropriate medical advice.

KITCHEN MAGIC

LAURA MAY

OVER 65 ENCHANTING RECIPES AND RITUALS FOR A COZY, WITCHY KITCHEN

ILLUSTRATIONS BY ROXY DEWAR
PHOTOGRAPHY BY ANDREW BURTON

OH

For all the wise women and witches who came before me,
who lit a path for me to follow.

CONTENTS

INTRODUCTION

One of the most magical times to be living on a narrowboat is the cusp of autumn. Like the transition from sleep to waking, it happens gently at first and then suddenly all at once. The soft patter of rain against the steel roof, the lake outside like a black glass mirror broken into circular shimmers by the raindrops, is shrouded in the mist of an autumn chill. The first day you wake up to the smell of burning wood, earthy damp leaves and rich soil – you know it's time. The whispers of winter are here, a stark contrast to the relentless summer sun that bathed the land in brightness just weeks ago. As I stir, I hear the geese overhead – their leaving calls echoing through the morning stillness, a reminder of the seasonal cycle that governs all life.

Autumn has arrived, and with it, the nostalgic ritual of relighting my fire. Each year the warmth of the fire feels like a familiar embrace, a sanctuary against the cold – and today, as I bake my ritual recipes in the stack stove, it will carry with it the weight of intention and magic. By the time I slide out of bed, the rain has stopped, but it has left a damp coldness in the air. Wrapping myself in a cozy jumper, I make my way to the tiny galley kitchen of my boat. Barely seven feet wide and only a few steps long, it's undoubtedly the heart of my floating home. My narrowboat may be small, but it holds infinite possibilities for a kitchen witch like me.

As I gather my logs and coal, sunlight filters through the window, casting a warm glow on my collection of herbs, magical trinkets and jars that line the shelves. The walls are laden with bunches of hanging plants, foraged throughout the year, now drying and ready to be used for something intentional, transformational – and tasty. These plants are trophies from a spring and summer filled with exploring folklore and magic through foraged food and creating some of my now favourite ritual recipes.

I stack the kindling in a criss-cross structure inside the belly of the stove and reach for one of my homemade firelighters. Fashioned from dried forest-floor flotsam and jetsam, wrapped diligently in discards of homemade paper, carefully tied with twine and sealed with wax – melted from the ends of used-up candles – these little creations are infused with my intentions. I choose one with orange wax for creativity, taking a moment to write a sigil on the paper, simple strokes forming a symbol that holds my will. I tuck it below the kindling and envision myself working hard today, creating recipes that can change paths through mindful intention, entwined with stories and wisdom from the ingredients I choose.

THE MAGIC OF RITUALS

As the flames settle into a steady burn, I turn my attention to my morning coffee ritual. This is a little practice I weave into every day. I reach for my moka pot, and as I prepare to brew my coffee, I decide to add something special. A pinch of dried yarrow, known for its properties of protection and getting you noticed, goes into the pot, mingling with the grounds.

With a flick of the match, I first light a purple candle to open the circle, a sign that my spell has begun. I then move my match to the hob. The blue gas flame catches, sending a warm glow dancing around the walls and charms of my little boat – gifts from friends, candles and keepsakes collected from my travels and experiences. It's easy to forget that this life I now cherish was once a dream – a far-off possibility that seemed unreachable. I'm still not sure what initiated my desire to live on a boat. It was something I yearned for many years before it happened, in the same way one might pine to go home to a place they had never been. Only after buying the boat did I discover that my grandparents had a narrowboat on the canals of the Midlands in the 60s, so perhaps it's in my blood.

As with most things in life, once you find the path you're supposed to be on, resistance tends to fall away – the current suddenly starts to flow your way when you're no longer swimming against it. In early 2020, I received the opportunity to make my dream a reality. I visited countless potential boats throughout the spring and summer hoping to find 'the one'. Six months and twelve boats later, I still hadn't felt that spark. I'd met some beautiful boats along the way, but none of them felt *right*, none of them felt like *mine*. I was starting to wonder if perhaps boat life was not meant for me after all.

In late September, on the autumn equinox, I held a dinner for friends and created a ritual recipe spell cake I like to call 'The Welcome Home Loaf' (see page 196). This cake is a vanilla chai sponge that contains clove and nutmeg for success, cinnamon for abundance, allspice for luck – and a key, baked into the body of the cake. As I shared this recipe with friends, we talked about how life would be once I found my narrowboat home – how it would impact their paths and mine. I plunged my fork into my slice of cake and hit something hard. I had unknowingly served myself the hidden key. A week later, I found my boat, *May Moon*. She was undoubtedly mine from the moment I set foot aboard.

KITCHEN WITCHERY

As the fire crackles, I add a log, the growing warmth now seeping into my bones, the stack stove oven above the fire almost warm enough for me to start creating. My practise was not always so rooted in food. I'd love to tell you that I come from a long line of women of the hearth, who passed their wisdom down to me, guiding pudgy hands into mixing bowls and telling folk stories imbued with the knowledge of our ancestors; that mothers and great aunts and grandmothers gathered around an heirloom wooden table and taught me how to knead intention into the bread with their paper stone hands. But this was not my experience.

A perfect storm of unbridled independence and an inherited tendency toward disordered eating and body shame were handed down to me as a child. My relationship with food has not always been a healthy one, but it is, in part, through kitchen magic that I found my recovery – a diet based on folklore and reconnection to natural wisdom and the earth beneath my feet. Healing on a more holistic level that encompasses connecting with others and myself. Where I once counted macros, I now look at how ingredients and the ritual of preparing them can bring my intentions into the physical as a recipe spell – adding magic into even the most seemingly mundane of meals. Kitchen witchery is by no means a replacement for the medical intervention I also received, but for me, it helped.

INTRODUCTION

A bowl of porridge is suddenly a recipe for bringing self-love into your morning routine. A chamomile moon milk can bring calm to the mind or ease period pain. A loaf of bread to share with friends can encompass thyme for courage and salt for protection. Each dish is more than sustenance; it's an opportunity to weave ceremony into your everyday. The philosophy behind my recipes is to give you a sense of meaning and consideration to everyday cooking – even the smallest acts can impact the way we live and see the world. These rituals aid us in discovering what we really want out of life and align our daily consciousness in order to get it. The stories and folk wisdom behind the ingredients teach us deep ancestral knowledge about the land, nature and how to move with it. We can experience food in a way that brings delight, not just through the eating, but also the connecting.

My moka pot starts to gargle and bubble, the steam beginning to rise, carrying with it the smell of the coffee brewing – a sign of the magic unfolding. I feel the connection between the elements, each one playing its part in the ritual. This is how I create my kitchen rituals – through intention, ceremony and bringing my desires into the physical.

I have a whole shelf of various homemade syrups, herbal mixes, vinegars, elixirs and oils, each one capturing the power of one or more magical ingredients. Cinnamon syrup for abundance, beetroot powder for grounding, dried chamomile for calming, rosemary oil for beauty, sage for wisdom, vanilla syrup for clarity – to name a few.

Today, I'm focused on creativity, as I'll be working on my book, this book that you hold in your hands. I want *Kitchen Magic* to shift how we think about food – not just as sustenance but also as a way to engage holistically with ourselves. Through these recipes, I aim to show you how to bring magic and intention into your everyday practice of cooking and eating. In these six chapters I want to help you connect not only with your food but with history, yourself, the world around you and with others.

WHAT'S AHEAD

In my first chapter, Folk Medicine, I pay homage to the early herbal practitioners who used food as medicine, laying the groundwork for the medicinal eating we are familiar with today. In Botanical Bakes, I dive into the folklore – both personal and historical – of seven of my favourite flowers and plants – telling their stories and sharing how their magic can be baked into your everyday. Ceremonial Recipes offers a seasonal journey through the Wheel of the Year, with food rituals that mark the turning points. In Menstrual Magic, I will show you not only how to soothe the symptoms of menstruation, but also how to harness their hidden powers. From alcohol alchemy to cauldron coffee, Broomstick Brews will show you how to make ritual potions of old – or simply change your daily coffee into an intention-setting spell. Lastly, you'll graduate to Practical Magic, taking everything you have learned from the previous chapters and setting it into a more complex ritualistic practice that encompasses the power of the moon and spoken word. These spell recipes bring solutions to some of life's most common challenges.

I reach for my vanilla (for clarity) and orange (for creativity) syrups for my coffee. The sharp sweetness weaving confidence, inspiration and concentration into the mixture – qualities I want to channel as I sip my drink and prepare for the day ahead.

I take my coffee over to the table and pull out my notebook and pen. I draft my to-do list, each task written with care. I'll be creating some new recipes today. Though it may seem more convenient to type the list out on my laptop, the tactile act of writing is a spell in itself – a commitment to bringing my thoughts to life. Studies show that written tasks are four times more likely to be completed, an example of magic that we often overlook. I believe in the power of rituals, not habits.

A gentle drizzle has started outside, but the sun continues to creep from behind the clouds. The caustic light reflections from the lake dance on my ceiling, a promise that even the dreariest days can hold beauty. In this life, on my floating home, I am not just a kitchen witch; I am a weaver of spells, a believer in the magic that exists within each of us, if we choose to see it.

As the fire crackles and the world outside shifts into autumn's vibrant tapestry, I am ready to embrace whatever magic this day holds.

WHAT IS A WITCH?

HAVE YOU EVER FELT A PULL TOWARD NATURE, TRUSTED YOUR INTUITION OVER LOGIC, OR SENSED SOMETHING 'IN YOUR WATERS'? IF SO, YOU MIGHT BE MORE IN TUNE WITH WITCHCRAFT THAN YOU THINK.

FOR YEARS, I HESITATED TO EMBRACE THE TERM 'WITCH'. IT FELT TOO LOADED, TOO TIED TO STEREOTYPES. BUT AS MY PRACTICE HAS EVOLVED, SO HAS MY UNDERSTANDING. WITCHCRAFT, FOR ME, IS MORE THAN SPELLS OR POINTY HATS – IT'S ABOUT CONNECTION, INTUITION AND GROUNDING MYSELF IN THE NATURAL WORLD.

Witchcraft is often misunderstood. People imagine witches with broomsticks, black cats or summoning dark forces. But in reality, it's more about personal power, healing and a deep respect for nature. Paganism and modern witchcraft practices, like Wicca, draw from ancient traditions, but they've evolved into something uniquely modern – an expression of spirituality that blends myth, folklore and ritual. For some, it's a religion. For others, it's a way to honour the cycles of life or tune into their natural intuition.

A common misconception is that witches aren't real, but history tells a different story. Women accused of witchcraft were often healers or those with knowledge of herbs and folk practices. They were feared and demonized, but their skills were necessary for survival. Many scholars now believe that the fear of witches wasn't just about superstition – it was also about control. In societies where women had little power, witchcraft became a way to vilify those who stepped outside the norm.

Today, witchcraft is a path many follow to regain a sense of agency in a chaotic world. It's about ritual and intention, whether it's lighting a candle, meditating or spending time in nature. These practices bring focus and mindfulness, helping us shape our lives in ways that feel more aligned with who we are.

Witchcraft doesn't need to be dramatic. It can be as simple as carrying a charm for luck or performing small rituals to manifest your intentions. These acts remind us that we have power over our lives, that we can influence our path through conscious effort. Whether you call it magic or mindfulness, it works because it shifts your perspective and sharpens your focus.

For me, being a witch is about balance and respect for the natural world. It's not about controlling others or bending the world to my will, but about living in harmony with the energies around us. It's about being connected to something bigger, knowing that while we can't control everything, we can shape how we respond. Witchcraft is more than superstition; it's a personal, spiritual journey that grounds us in the present and empowers us to face the future with intention.

It should also be noted that 'witchcraft' is not limited to a specific culture or geography – magical practices exist all across the globe in one form or another, and we should endeavour not to homogenize them all into one singular thing. There are some similarities and equivalent ideas found within these folk practices, however much of my personal practice, which I share within the pages of this recipe grimoire, is rooted in Celtic and European pagan ideas: folklore and folk magic from the British Isles, festivals and traditions largely from England, Ireland, Scotland and Wales. Anyone can connect to this wisdom, irrespective of where you live, and although the teachings should ultimately be treated with reverence and respect for the cultures from which they come, you do not need to identify as a witch or a pagan to explore and benefit from the magic within.

THE ORIGIN OF THE 'WITCH'

THE FIGURE OF THE WITCH HAS BEEN HELD WITH FEAR AND FASCINATION IN EQUAL MEASURE FOR CENTURIES. FROM DARK FOLK TALES OF SORCERY, HYSTERIA AND PERSECUTION TO POP CULTURE'S DEPICTION OF THE GREEN-SKINNED, WART-FACED HAG. MANY HAVE RECLAIMED THE CLASSIC ICONOGRAPHY OF THE WITCH AS SYMBOLS OF EMPOWERMENT AND REBELLION BUT, ALTHOUGH THE WAY WITCHES ARE VIEWED MAY BE EVOLVING, CERTAIN SYMBOLS REMAIN THE SAME. BROOMSTICKS, CAULDRONS, POINTY HATS, CATS, CANDLES AND INCENSE ARE MORE THAN AESTHETIC – THEY EACH CARRY A PROFOUND HISTORICAL, CULTURAL AND PRACTICAL SIGNIFICANCE.

THE BROOMSTICK

The broomstick, or besom (a traditional broom made of twigs bound to a stick), is a powerful symbol of cleansing and renewal. Historically, it became linked with witches due to its everyday presence in homes and its use in fertility rituals. To me, my broomstick is not just symbolic; it's practical. Before I cook, I sweep my kitchen with intention, imagining negativity and stagnant energy being brushed away, making space for growth and renewal. Many witches find this ritual grounding. Creating a besom with twigs and herbs adds another layer of meaning to this timeless tool.

THE CAULDRON AND POINTY HATS

The cauldron, a powerful symbol of transformation and renewal, has roots in ancient myths, such as the Celtic cauldron of inspiration and rebirth. Traditionally, it was a vessel of magic, but in practise, any pot can become your 'cauldron'. I often use mine to simmer stews, teas, or other comforting creations, combining ingredients with care and purpose. This simple act feels like a ritual, reminding me that nourishment – both physical and spiritual – is deeply interconnected. Magic often arises from the everyday when approached with intention.

Medieval alewives, skilled women brewers, also relied on cauldrons as they crafted beer in their homes. Their pointed hats (which made them easy to spot in crowded marketplaces) and brewing tools and eventually became tied to the imagery of witchcraft, as brewing transitioned to a male-dominated industry. Their stories inspire me when I work with yeasts or fermentations, honouring these women who provided sustenance for their communities despite significant societal challenges. The cauldron, both a symbol and a tool, connects us to these historic figures while inviting us to embrace everyday alchemy in our kitchens.

CATS

Cats, particularly black ones, are iconic witch familiars (animal companions of witches that assist with magic and protection). Pope Gregory IX's decree in the 13th century tied them to witchcraft, leading to mass exterminations. Ironically, this worsened the plague as rats flourished. For me, cats have always been soulful companions. Many witches feel a deep affinity with animals, especially those, like cats, who embody mystery and independence.

CANDLES AND INCENSE

Candles and incense are ancient tools for focus and cleansing the space of negative energy. I use candles to hold space and open the circle during rituals. Burning herbs or resins connects me to universal practices of renewal and intention-setting. I avoid terms like 'smudging', respecting its sacredness to indigenous cultures, and instead use the term 'cleansing'.

THE CORE PRINCIPLES OF RITUAL

RITUALS, MUCH LIKE RECIPES, ARE WONDERFULLY FLEXIBLE AND ADAPTABLE. EACH ONE IS MADE UP OF ELEMENTS THAT CAN BE ADDED, ADJUSTED OR SIMPLIFIED DEPENDING ON YOUR NEEDS OR INTENTIONS. JUST AS ONE RECIPE MAY CALL UPON A COMPLICATED VARIETY OF INGREDIENTS WITH ELABORATE STEPS, ANOTHER MAY BENEFIT FROM SIMPLICITY. A SINGLE CANDLE, ONE SPOKEN WORD, A MINDFUL STIR IN THE RIGHT DIRECTION – EACH ELEMENT CAN BRING MAGIC INTO ANY RECIPE. THE MORE A RITUAL IS TAILORED TO YOUR SPECIFIC INTENTIONS, THE MORE POWERFUL IT WILL BE.

OPENING THE CIRCLE

Lighting a candle before you start cooking (or eating) is an act of 'opening the circle'. This simply means that you are ready to set your intention. Some people like to open their circle by saying a few words or acknowledging each element in some way. I personally don't find it necessary to open a circle every time I cook a recipe (especially if I'm baking something that takes hours of prep and proving), but this act might come later – for example during the kneading, decorating or even when I eat the food and focus mindfully on the intention I'm setting. Blowing out the candle is also a way of closing the circle – the intention has been set and the smoke carries it out into the universe for you.

CANDLE COLOURS

Candle magic is an ancient practice, and each colour corresponds to a different type of energy, making it a powerful tool in your kitchen rituals. When adding this layer to your spells, consider the following colours and their meanings:

White: Purity, cleansing, protection, general-purpose.
Black: Banishing negativity, protection, endings.
Red: Passion, courage, strength.
Orange: Creativity, joy, enthusiasm.
Yellow: Confidence, communication, mental clarity.
Green: Abundance, growth, prosperity.
Blue: Calm, healing, communication.
Purple: Spirituality, intuition, intellect, power.
Pink: Love, friendship, self-care.

You can use these candles when performing your kitchen magic, aligning your intentions with the energy each colour represents.

MOON PHASES

Though I don't specify moon phases for each recipe (other than those in Practical Magic), they can add another layer of potency to your ritual cooking.

The moon's energy affects everything from tides to emotions, and aligning your recipes with the lunar cycle can enhance their effectiveness. For example, the new moon is ideal for setting intentions, waxing moon for growth and manifestation, full moon for completion, gratitude and celebration, and waning moon for banishing or releasing.

Feel free to tailor your cooking around these phases to heighten your ritual. If you're baking bread for abundance, a waxing moon may help that intention grow with more strength, for example.

SIGILS

A sigil is a symbol infused with your intention. They are highly customizable and can be used in food magic in many creative ways. One form of making a sigil is this; start by writing down your intention (e.g., 'grounding' or 'abundance'). Then, break it down into letters written atop one another to create a unique symbol that represents your desire.

I often write sigils onto bay leaves and toss them into soups and stews, or even bake them into dough. You can use a food-safe pen, food colouring and a brush or even a little lemon juice for this. The bay leaf carries the intention through the cooking process, infusing the dish with your specific magical focus. Once it is cooked, you can remove the bay leaf. You may choose to let it dry and mindfully burn it later, letting the smoke carry your intention to the sky.

INTENTIONAL STIRRING

One of the simplest yet most effective forms of kitchen witchery is stirring with intention. When you stir clockwise, you invite energies in – such as love, abundance or healing. When you stir anticlockwise, you banish or release them – such as stress, negativity or obstacles. This method is an easy way to add a subtle yet powerful magical act into any dish, from soups to sauces to herbal teas.

SPOKEN WORD

The spoken word plays a central role in magic and spell casting, acting as a conduit between intention and manifestation. Language shapes our perception and can influence reality. Historically, cultures believed that words carried power – whether in the form of incantations, chants or affirmations. The act of vocalizing a spell transforms abstract desires into tangible energy. The Old English word 'spel', meaning speech or story, highlights the deep connection between language and magic. When we speak a spell or chant, we are not merely communicating, but actively shaping the world around us. By vocalizing our intentions, we direct energy, influencing outcomes in both the physical and spiritual realms. This principle is reflected in modern practices like affirmations, which harness the power of words to influence mindset and create change. Thus, spoken words are not just symbolic; they are transformative, bridging the gap between thought and reality.

ELEMENTAL MAGIC

When cooking, you're already working with the four classical elements – Earth (ingredients), Water (liquids), Fire (heat) and Air (steam, breath, spoken word). You can intentionally align with these elements to enhance your kitchen witchcraft.

Earth: Represents grounding and nourishment. Root vegetables, grains and hearty stews tap into Earth's energy.
Water: Purification and emotional healing. Use it consciously when preparing broths, teas or infusions.
Fire: Transformation and passion. Cooking with heat, roasting, lighting a candle or adding spices like chilli invoke Fire's transformative power.
Air: Intellect and communication. Intentional stirring or spoken word invites Air into your rituals.

GATHERING NATURE

FOR MANY WITCHES, THE CENTRAL FOCUS OF THEIR PRACTICE IS GROUNDED IN THEIR RELATIONSHIP WITH THE NATURAL WORLD. BEING LUCKY ENOUGH TO GROW UP LARGELY IN THE COUNTRYSIDE MEANT THAT MY CHILDHOOD DAYS WERE SPENT PADDLING IN BROOKS AND STREAMS, GETTING STUCK IN THE MUD, BUILDING DENS, FASHIONING BOWS AND ARROWS OR LEAF BOATS AND RUNNING THROUGH MEADOWS AND FIELDS WITH WILD ABANDON.

I was truly a feral child, my knees always bruised, dirt under every nail, and arms tattooed with nettle stings and bramble scratches. Nature was my playground, and it taught me so much. My favourite memories from childhood are simply being alone in nature – meeting cows, exploring woodlands and indulging a peaceful fascination with being at one with the earth. The first time I tentatively plucked something from the earth with intention to eat it was when I was around nine. Nettles are a plant that we are all instinctually familiar with from a young age because we all learn early that they sting – and the hot itchy prickle leaves an impression which makes it very easy to identify. When I learned that, once cooked, these pain-inducing plants can be eaten I was fascinated! Most of us go blackberry and damson picking as children, but this was the first time I felt I had discovered some knowledge and put it into practice on my own. The nettles, of course, did not taste good, despite being stewed and drowned with sweet honey in an attempt to make them palatable. You couldn't really call it a recipe and you certainly couldn't call it successful, but it left such a lasting impression on me.

My sacred dens were a place of escapism. In a world of my own I was living in a tree den, with chairs made of cut logs, curtains of ivy for privacy and soft beds of dry fallen leaves – the idea that I could also sustain myself using what I could find in the hedgerows was thrilling. I wanted to be a life-sized 'borrower', taking from the land instead of people – utilizing sticks and stones instead of sewing box buttons. I wanted to be resourceful but still frivolous. I wasn't interested in my sewing and fire-making Scout badges from a survival perspective, but from one of living luxuriously in nature. A realistic notion? Perhaps not, but I didn't want realism, I longed for a storybook setting to indulge my imagination in.

My boat is the culmination of this longing for a place of my own. I may not have bricks or mortar – or more importantly, land – something which is hard to obtain in England, but my boat is my den.

Prior to living on the boat, I found the solace of nature in pockets of London. Zone 2 might not sound like the most green-space-filled place, but the wetlands, towpaths and local cemetery provided me with all I needed – is was proof that foraging and connecting to nature is not just for those lucky enough to live deep in the countryside. With its parks and gardens and even farms (yes, farms!), London is an incredibly biodiverse city.

My local spot was Tower Hamlets Cemetery Park. Each day I explored, I seemed to find something new to research and eat. I developed an almost instinctual knack about which plants looked edible and which did not. Some called me to pick them, and others screamed danger with just a look. I would do heavy research and identification before eating anything – there are many books, websites and resources to identify wild plants and flowers. There are even websites dedicated to foraging specifically in cities – for many, urban living doesn't need to be a barrier to connecting to wild food.

During the pandemic, I'm sure that most of us had a local spot to wander that we cherished – Cemetery Park was mine and I trod the earth almost every day. I found stitchwort, wild lemon balm and mint, honeysuckle, Queen Anne's lace, fireweed, garlic mustard, wild garlic, sweet woodruff, heartsease, cowslip, green alkanet, borage, comfrey, wild dead nettle, stinging nettles, wild strawberries, honesty, mugwort, sorrel and many, many more. Further afield, along the canal towpaths I found gorse, fennel and mallow, and Victoria Park gave me dandelions, chickweed and sweet violet.

FORAGING PRACTICE

The way I see it, gathering food is our oldest, most primal relationship to the earth and 'wildcrafting' (transforming the raw elements of nature into food, drink and medicine) is the world's oldest magic. From spring to summer, autumn to winter, I revive the ancient culinary arts of bringing blessings to ourselves, our families, communities, and to our Great Mother, the Earth, one delicious bite at a time.

Although it can be tempting to feel entitled to all this 'free' food, I would be remiss if I encouraged you to go out and gather without first mentioning the importance of responsible foraging. After living by Cemetery Park and exploring its growing goods throughout the seasons for a few years, I was horrified in early 2020 when I went out to collect some wild garlic and found that the carpet of green on the forest floor had been absolutely ransacked. The lawn of abundant leaves had all been freshly beheaded, leaving behind nothing but a cluster of white stumpy stems. In the corner was a crouching figure huddled with bags and bags of it. Cutting and stuffing, cutting and stuffing – without care or respect. It was only when the plastic carrier bags were bulging that they went on their way, leaving nothing left. I learned later that this was the work of commercial restaurants taking it for their highly priced 'forest to table' dishes. I love the idea of people connecting to the land through wild food – but something about this rubbed me the wrong way.

There are some rules I like to follow to ensure responsible and respectful foraging:

- When gathering, it's best to only take what you need.
- Make sure you have the right permission if you're on someone else's property, and above all, silently seek permission from the plant itself – a simple act of acknowledgment that shows you understand and respect the balance between taking and gratitude.
- For most plants, it's not ideal to dig up the root or bulb; we want to give it the chance to grow again next year.
- It's best to only pick from plentiful patches, and leave enough behind for others, the insects and animals. I like to be particularly lenient with the flowers favoured by bees.
- Don't pick anything rare or protected.
- Lastly, be confident in your identification – you'd be surprised how many unassuming plants and flowers are toxic or even deadly, and how similar they can look to their innocuous or edible counterparts!

The availability of wild plants will differ depending on season and location. The Further Reading section (see page 203) has book recommendations on foraging so that you can be confident in your identification.

THE WITCH'S STORE CUPBOARD

THE PROPERTIES OF YOUR HERBS, SPICES AND INGREDIENTS

WITHIN THE WITCH'S STORE CUPBOARD, YOU WILL FIND CERTAIN STAPLES THAT ARE INTEGRAL TO THEIR PRACTICE. FOR THE KITCHEN WITCH THESE WILL RANGE FROM HANGING HERBS TO MOON WATER TO SALT AND PEPPER. IN FACT, WITCH OR NOT, YOU'LL PROBABLY FIND THAT YOU HAVE A GOOD NUMBER OF THESE INGREDIENTS IN YOUR PANTRY ALREADY!

These are the elements you will come back to time and time again. Many of them have meanings and attributes that add to the potency of an intention – even if they are not the main symbolic ingredient of a dish. Yeast, for example, is all about rising and growing. Baking, therefore, is ideal for spells of abundance, manifestation and 'bringing in' (inviting things into your life, such as new habits and changes).

Each ingredient matters, not only for taste, but also for intention, no matter how small. It is by using these symbolic connections that you can create ritual recipe spells of your own. This is also a good list to create substitutions from. If an intention seems particularly lofty or complicated, you can condense the essence into a simple moon milk or cake. Have a look at this glossary of magical properties for some inspiration.

ALLSPICE

Properties: Money, luck, healing.
Folklore: Allspice is associated with abundance and healing, and is used in Caribbean folk magic to attract money and good fortune.

APPLE

Properties: Garden magic, love, healing, vanity, marriage, beauty.
Folklore: Apples are linked to abundance, enhancing beauty and attracting love, particularly during the autumn equinox and Samhain.

BASIL

Properties: Love, protection, prosperity.
Folklore: Basil symbolizes love in Italian folklore and is sacred in Hinduism. It's used to attract prosperity and divine protection.

BAY LEAVES

Properties: Protection, success, divination, manifestation.
Folklore: Sacred to Apollo in ancient Greece and Rome, bay leaves were used in rituals for protection, success and to ensure victory. They can add potency to any manifestation recipe.

BLACK PEPPER

Properties: Protection, banishment, warding off negativity, adding speed.
Folklore: Black pepper repels unwanted energies and helps to accelerate results, bringing about desired changes quickly.

MOON WATER

MOON WATER IS WATER THAT HAS BEEN CHARGED BY THE ENERGY OF THE MOON. YOU CAN CAPTURE THIS ENERGY BY LEAVING A GLASS JAR OF WATER OUTSIDE OVERNIGHT TO SOAK UP THE MOONLIGHT. WATER CHARGED BY THE DIFFERENT PHASES OF THE MOON CAN BE USED TO REPRESENT DIFFERENT THINGS IN YOUR RITUAL RECIPES.

CARAWAY

Properties: Protection, fidelity, health.
Folklore: Caraway seeds are used to ensure fidelity in lovers and protect against illness and negative energies.

CARDAMOM

Properties: Love, clarity, protection.
Folklore: Valued in Indian and Middle Eastern traditions, cardamom is used in love spells and for mental clarity, also offering protection.

CINNAMON

Properties: Prosperity, love, protection.
Folklore: Cinnamon was highly valued for attracting wealth and enhancing love and protection, especially in ancient Egypt and Rome.

COCOA AND CHOCOLATE

Properties: Love, passion, energy.
Folklore: Cocoa was revered by the Aztecs, used in rituals to invoke love, fertility and vitality.

CUMIN

Properties: Protection, fidelity, love.
Folklore: Cumin is believed to promote fidelity and protect against theft when sprinkled around the home, acting as a 'keeper'.

DATES

Properties: Fertility, health, abundance.
Folklore: Dates symbolize fertility and prosperity, and are consumed to promote health and ensure a bountiful life.

FENUGREEK

Properties: Wealth, health, fertility.
Folklore: Fenugreek was used in ancient Egypt and the Middle East to enhance wealth, fertility and healing.

FLOUR

Properties: Abundance, prosperity, protection.
Folklore: Flour symbolizes abundance and prosperity, and is used in rituals to ensure a bountiful harvest and financial stability.

GARLIC

Properties: Protection, purification, healing.
Folklore: Garlic is renowned for warding off evil spirits and protecting homes; it's often hung in doorways for its protective qualities.

GINGER

Properties: Energy, success, protection.
Folklore: Ginger boosts vitality and attracts prosperity. It's included in spells to speed up results and enhance success.

JUNIPER

Properties: Protection, guards against theft.
Folklore: Juniper was hung on doors to protect against evil and ne'er-do-wells. It is believed to break hexes and ward off snakes.

LEGUMES

Properties: Prosperity, protection, sustenance.
Folklore: Legumes, especially black-eyed peas, are eaten on New Year's Day in the Southern US to bring good fortune and protection.

LEMONS

Properties: Purification, love, healing.
Folklore: Lemons were used in Mediterranean traditions to ward off evil spirits, and they are also associated with purification and healing.

LEMON BALM

Properties: Eases stress, increases intelligence, healing, protection, love.
Folklore: Lemon balm reduces stress, enhances intelligence and provides healing and protection, also attracting love.

LEMON VERBENA

Properties: Draws love, attracts money, luck, enhances psychic ability.
Folklore: Lemon verbena attracts love and money, brings luck and enhances psychic abilities.

MARIGOLD

Properties: Healing, protection, justice, love, prosperity, creativity.
Folklore: Marigolds are used for healing, protection and promoting justice, love and creativity. They are particularly associated with Lammas.

MILK

Properties: Nourishment, purity, prosperity.
Folklore: Milk symbolizes nourishment and purity. In Hindu rituals, it's used to invoke prosperity and cleanse the soul.

MINT

Properties: Healing, protection, prosperity.
Folklore: Mint is used to heal, protect and attract prosperity. It is also used in ancient Greek funeral rites.

NIGELLA SEED

Properties: Protection, health, prosperity.
Folklore: Known as 'the seed of blessing' in the Middle East, nigella seeds offer protection and attract health and prosperity.

NUTMEG

Properties: Luck, money, health.
Folklore: In the Middle Ages, nutmeg was used to attract wealth and ward off illness, symbolizing good fortune and health.

OATS

Properties: Prosperity, grounding, health.
Folklore: Oats are used in Celtic traditions for health and prosperity; they are associated with grounding energy and physical wellness.

OLIVE OIL

Properties: Peace, healing, protection.
Folklore: Olive oil is used in Mediterranean rituals for anointing, healing and ensuring peace, symbolizing divine protection.

ONION

Properties: Protection, purification, healing.
Folklore: Onions are used as protective talismans, believed to absorb negative energy and safeguard against evil.

POTATOES

Properties: Protection, grounding, healing.
Folklore: Potatoes are believed to absorb negative energy and protect homes from curses, symbolizing grounding and healing.

RICE

Properties: Prosperity, fertility, protection.
Folklore: Rice symbolizes life and fertility in many Asian cultures, and so it is used to bless weddings and protect the future.

HAVE YOU HEARD THE OLD WIVES' TALE THAT THUNDERSTORMS CURDLE MILK? IT TURNS OUT THAT WHILE MILK OFTEN WENT BAD DURING STORMS, IT WASN'T DUE TO LIGHTNING. IN THE 19TH CENTURY, THEORIES SUGGESTED THAT ELECTRICITY OR OZONE MIGHT BE TO BLAME. HOWEVER, SCIENTISTS LATER FOUND THAT BACTERIA, THRIVING IN WARM, HUMID CONDITIONS, WERE THE REAL CULPRITS. PASTEURIZATION AND REFRIGERATION HAVE SINCE DEBUNKED THE MYTH, THOUGH SOME STILL BELIEVE IN THE CONNECTION, ESPECIALLY WHERE RAW MILK IS CONSUMED.

ROSEMARY

Properties: Memory, protection, love, purification.
Folklore: Rosemary is used in rituals for protection and love, and is associated with memory and purification.

SAGE

Properties: Wisdom, protection, purification.
Folklore: Sage is used for cleansing, protection and enhancing wisdom; it's often paired with rosemary for added spiritual strength.

SALT

Properties: Purification, protection, warding off evil.
Folklore: Salt is used in various cultures for protection against evil spirits and bad luck; it's often used to cleanse environments and safeguard spaces.

SEAWEED

Properties: Protection, prosperity, health.
Folklore: Seaweed is used in Celtic and Norse traditions to protect against misfortune and attract prosperity; used in coastal rituals.

SUGAR

Properties: Love, attraction, sweetness.
Folklore: Sugar is used in love spells to sweeten feelings and attract love. It symbolizes joy and hospitality.

THYME

Properties: Courage, purification, health.
Folklore: Thyme was used by ancient Greeks to imbue warriors with bravery and vitality. It's also used for purification and health.

TURMERIC

Properties: Purification, healing, protection.
Folklore: Turmeric is used in Hindu rituals for cleansing and protection, its vibrant colour symbolizing healing and spiritual reverence.

VANILLA

Properties: Love, passion, mental clarity.
Folklore: Used to invoke love, sensuality and mental clarity.

VINEGAR

Properties: Purification, protection, preservation.
Folklore: Vinegar is associated with purification and protection, and is used to cleanse spaces and ward off negative energies.

WORMWOOD

Properties: Protection, divination, dreams, exorcism.
Folklore: Wormwood is used for protection, enhancing divination, and aiding in dreams and exorcisms.

YEAST

Properties: Transformation, growth, abundance.
Folklore: Yeast represents transformation and abundance as it makes bread rise, symbolizing growth and life.

A NOTE ON INGREDIENTS

All of these recipes will work whether you stick to a vegan, vegetarian or omnivorous diet. The aim is to make them as accessible as possible, no matter what your personal diet is. All of the recipes are egg-free and there are very few where you will need something that isn't generally in everyone's cupboard. The recipes will work whether you are choosing dairy or non-dairy milk, butter, cheese and cream – it all comes down to your personal choice.

A NOTE ON MEASUREMENTS

US measurements are given in cups unless pounds and ounces are deemed more accurate.

KITCHEN WITCHERY IS ALL ABOUT TASTE AND INTENTION, SO SUBBING OUT INGREDIENTS YOU CAN'T FIND FOR THEIR COMMON COUNTERPART IS ABSOLUTELY FINE! A PINCH OF THIS, A DASH OF THAT – WHATEVER TASTES GREAT AND EFFECTIVELY SOWS YOUR INTENTION INTO THE DISH. GET CREATIVE AND HAVE FUN!

FOLK MEDICINE

HEALING RECIPES OF OLD AND THEIR ORIGINS

Ancient civilisations relied on observations, trial and error, and passed-down wisdom to identify plants that could alleviate pain or treat illness. This knowledge was transmitted orally, intertwined with stories, becoming the foundation of all medicine. For example, meadowsweet, revered in ancient herbal traditions as a pain reliever, was key to developing aspirin.

In Europe, folk medicine was deeply intertwined with rural life. Herbalism and midwifery played vital roles in managing health issues, particularly before formal medical education was widespread. Likewise, indigenous cultures across the Americas, Africa and Australia closely tied folk medicine to spirituality and environmental knowledge.

While some traditional cures may seem nonsensical, they often contain kernels of wisdom. Preserving and respecting these healing traditions can foster a sense of community and cultural heritage, offering continuity in a rapidly changing society and empowering people who feel disconnected.

Food and folklore are intrinsically linked – showing us not only the wisdom of plants, but also the stories and knowledge of our ancestors. The recipes we inherit are much more than mere instructions – they are narratives that connect us to our cultural heritage, local traditions and the natural landscape around us.

Just as folklore varies from one region to another, so too do the recipes, weaving together a rich and unique tapestry of the environment of each place they were made. The act of preparing and sharing food is a way to honour these traditions – to remember the lessons of the past and to connect with the rhythms of nature.

FOUR THIEVES' VINEGAR

A TONIC FOR PROTECTION

As the Black Death ravaged its way across medieval Europe, people desperately looked for solutions and treatments to prevent and remedy the effects of the disease. These antidotes ranged from harmless superstitions, such as carrying charms and amulets for protection, to practices that are painfully ironic knowing the modern science of how viral diseases actually work. They included bloodletting, which only weakened already ailing patients, and the use of toxic substances such as arsenic and mercury – believed to purge the body of disease but which instead caused severe poisoning. Added to this, they not only executed 'witches', who were believed to be one of the causes of the plague, but also their cats – a natural predator of the rats, whose fleas actually were spreading it.

Some remedies and treatments, however, have since been proven to have an effective backing in science and would certainly have had some positive effect on staving off the infection. Four Thieves' Vinegar is one of the latter and was the tonic du jour of medieval Europe. Named after a legend of four thieves who used it to protect themselves against plague while they robbed the dead or dying, it was traditionally used as a disinfectant or immunity tonic. Its uses today are still applicable as both a tonic and even a natural disinfectant. This mixture can be used as the base for a salad dressing, you can take a spoonful a day as a health tonic, or you can even put it in a spray bottle and use as an eco-friendly cleaning spray! Feel free to design your own tonic around your preferences.

MAKES 500ML (17FL OZ)

2 tbsp dried rosemary
2 tbsp dried thyme
2 tbsp dried sage
2 tbsp dried peppermint
9 garlic cloves, crushed
1 tsp black peppercorns
1 cinnamon stick
1 lemon, zest and juice
500ml (2 cups) apple cider vinegar

Add all of your aromatic ingredients to a sterile jar and pour the vinegar over to fully submerge. Place a cloth or piece of baking parchment under the lid if your lid is metal, as the vinegar will react with metal. Close the jar tightly and shake well. Store in a cool dry place for 2–4 weeks, shaking daily (or near enough).

Strain the mixture through a fine mesh strainer or cheese cloth, then pour the liquid into a sterile bottle or jar. Stored in a cool dark place it will keep for 6–12 months. While it is not necessary, refrigeration can help to maintain freshness.

IT'S THOUGHT THAT FOUR THIEVES' VINEGAR WAS IN FACT RELATIVELY HELPFUL IN PROTECTING AGAINST THE PLAGUE, SIMPLY BECAUSE IT WOULD KEEP PLAGUE-CARRYING FLEAS AT BAY. SO ALTHOUGH TONICS AND REMEDIES FROM THE PAST MIGHT SEEM FANTASTICAL, THERE OFTEN TURNS OUT TO BE METHOD IN THE MADNESS!

FIRE CIDER

A POWERFUL IMMUNITY TONIC

This traditional herbal remedy, popularized by renowned herbalist Rosemary Gladstar in the 1980s, is a potent blend of immune-boosting, warming ingredients. Often viewed as a herbal tonic, fire cider has been passed down through generations in folk and herbal medicine, symbolizing cultural heritage and personal empowerment. However, this cherished remedy faced an unprecedented threat when a corporate entity attempted to trademark the name – a pretty audacious move for a recipe they did not name or create. On one side stood passionate herbalists and small businesses advocating for the right to share their traditional knowledge freely – they understood that fire cider is more than just a recipe; it embodies a sense of community, connection, accessible health for all and shared wisdom. On the opposing side was a corporation trying to commodify and gatekeep this folk remedy for profit, attempting to restrict access to something that inherently belonged to the people. Fortunately, the tides turned in favour of the herbal community and, at least for now, fire cider remains in the hands of those who cherish it – everyday folk. A lesson that some things simply can't be owned; they belong to the collective spirit of those who treasure them.

MAKES 500–700ML (17–24FL OZ)

50g (1¾oz) **grated horseradish root**
50g (1¾oz) **chopped onion**
10 garlic cloves, minced
50g (1¾oz) **ginger root, grated**
½ tsp cayenne pepper
2 tbsp ground turmeric (or 5cm/2in fresh turmeric root, grated)
1 lemon, zest and juice
1 orange, zest and juice
2 sprigs of fresh rosemary
2 sprigs of fresh thyme
2 tbsp maple syrup (optional)
500–700ml (2–3 cups) **raw apple cider vinegar** (enough to cover the ingredients)

Add all of your aromatic ingredients to a sterile jar. Fire cider is incredibly adaptable to preference – add what you like/have and leave out what you don't. Pour the vinegar over to cover, then close the jar tightly and shake well. (Place a cloth or baking parchment under metal lids when making vinegar mixtures as vinegar will corrode the metal.) Store in a cool dry place – giving it a good shake everyday (or if you're anything like me, every few days when you remember). After 2–3 weeks you can strain away the solid ingredients and sweeten with a spoon of maple syrup if desired.

You can use this for a daily shot – it will last for 6 months whether stored in the fridge or a cool dark place (though it should be checked for spoilage). I add it to soups, smoothies or even cocktails!

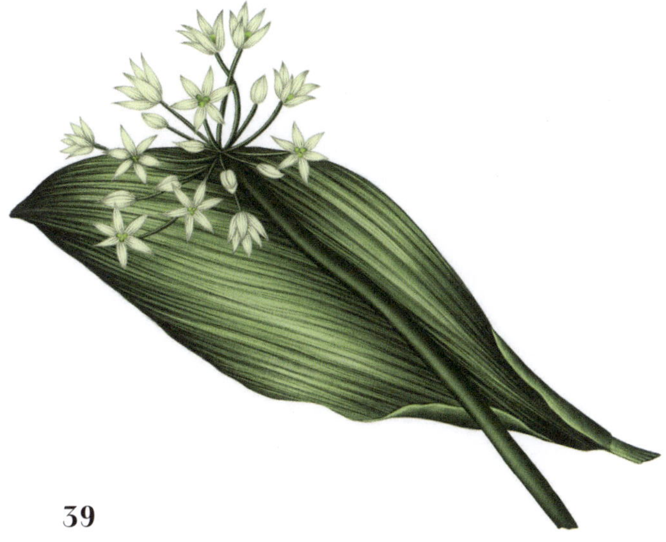

ELDERBERRY COUGH SYRUP

TO TREAT AND PREVENT WINTER ILLS

The elder tree, with its sweet, fragrant flowers, holds a special place in European traditions. It is believed to be protected by fairy folk and to house malevolent spirits within its hollow trunk. The deep red berries serve as a warning to those who might harm the tree, symbolizing both vengeance and justice. Cutting down an elder tree is said to bring misfortune, reflecting the deep respect our ancestors had for nature. Woodcutters in rural England would recite rhymes to Mother Elder to ward off spirits when harvesting from the tree. Legend tells that the children of witches were buried beneath its roots, re-emerging as butterflies, bees and caterpillars. The elder is associated with protection and justice – and befriending it offers rewards. Its berries contain antiviral properties that boost the immune system, helping fend off colds, flus and coughs while speeding recovery. Despite its fearsome reputation, the elder tree offers powerful healing to those who treat it with respect. This traditional recipe, essentially nature's cough syrup, not only treats colds, flus and coughs, but can prevent them as well.

MAKES 500–600ML (17–21FL OZ)

100g (3½oz) fresh and clean elderberries (or 25g/1oz dried)
1 cinnamon stick
1 tbsp grated fresh ginger (or 1 tsp ground ginger)
200ml (¾ cup) maple syrup
1 tbsp lemon juice

Combine the elderberries, cinnamon stick and ginger in a saucepan with 500ml (2 cups) water. Simmer over a low–medium heat for 45 minutes – the liquid should reduce by half and thicken slightly. Let it cool, then strain the mixture through a fine mesh strainer into a bowl. You may want to add the cooled remnants into a cheesecloth to squeeze out as much liquid as possible with your hands. At this point, add the maple syrup and lemon juice.

Pour the syrup into a sterilized glass jar or bottle and store in the fridge. This will keep for up to 6 months. Take it daily for protection or use it as needed to soothe colds and flus.

YARROW AND BLACKBERRY OXYMEL

AN ANTI-INFLAMMATORY TONIC

Yarrow, also known as 'Soldier's Woundwort' and 'Knight's Milfoil', has a rich history of use in treating battlefield injuries, due to its ability to slow or stop bleeding. Along with mugwort, yarrow was used to regulate menstruation and played a role in wedding rituals, where it was consumed to ensure marriages lasted at least seven years. It was used in ancient divination practices, known as 'yarrow stalk divination', to predict the future and was also hung in doorways and placed in cradles to ward off evil spirits. Yarrow and blackberries, both known for their potent medicinal properties, are ideal ingredients for an oxymel – a type of herbal remedy dating back to ancient Greece and Rome. Traditionally made by combining vinegar and honey (or, in this case, maple syrup), oxymels extract and preserve the medicinal qualities of herbs. These sweet and sour elixirs are far more palatable than other tonics and tinctures, truly living up to the phrase, 'helping the medicine go down!' This yarrow and blackberry oxymel is a time-honoured remedy, commonly used for immune support, soothing sore throats and promoting overall health. Yarrow offers anti-inflammatory benefits, while blackberries provide a rich source of antioxidants – making this a powerful, yet pleasant, traditional tonic.

MAKES 400ml (14fl oz)

50g (1¾oz) fresh (or 2 tbsp dried) yarrow leaves and flowers
100g (3½oz) fresh blackberries
250ml (1 cup) apple cider vinegar
100ml (scant ½ cup) maple syrup

Place your yarrow and blackberries into a clean sterilized jar. Pour the apple cider vinegar and maple syrup on top, making sure that everything is submerged. Store in a cool dark place for 2–4 weeks, shaking and burping by taking the lid off to release gas occasionally.

Once ready, strain the liquid into a sterile jar or bottle, pressing out as much liquid as possible. This will keep in the fridge for up to 6 months. I recommend taking a tablespoon daily in a tea, smoothie or just straight up!

SACRED HERBS SIMMER POT

A CLEANSING, PROTECTIVE RITUAL

This recipe is inspired by the Saxon Nine Herbs Charm, a medicinal spell from the 10th-century Old English text, *Lacnunga*. It invokes nine herbs and was used as a remedy for infections and wounds. The charm combines early medieval medical knowledge with pagan rituals, using both practical herbal remedies and magical incantations. The herbs were thought to possess healing powers and the charm's recitation helped ward off evil spirits or diseases.

The recitation invokes each herb by name, often addressing the herb directly, asking it to banish illness and protect a person. The combination of herbology and verbal charm reflects Anglo-Saxon medicinal practices blending magic and medicine. You can use dried or fresh herbs, or a mix of either for this. It should be noted that it is not advisable for pregnant women to ingest mugwort.

MAKES 900ML (30FL OZ)

A handful of fresh (or 2 tbsp dried) of each of the following:
Mugwort (protection, healing)
Plantain (healing)
Chamomile (calming, healing)
Nettle (purification, protection)
Betony (healing)
Lamb's Cress (purification)
Crab Apple (fertility, protection)
Chervil (healing)
Fennel (protection, strength)

To a large pot of boiling water, add each ingredient one by one – saying its name and asking for protection. Simmer for 30 minutes, filling your home with their healing aroma.

Strain and use the liquid as a tea, add to a bath for healing, or even mop the floor with it to protect your home!

MEDIEVAL CURES RANGE FROM LYING ON A SHILLING TO CURE HICCUPS, TO APPLYING OINTMENTS TO WEAPONS THAT HAVE INFLICTED WOUNDS, TO DABBING VINEGAR AND URINE ON ONES FACE TO REMOVE FRECKLES.

BOTANICAL BAKES

FROM ANCIENT GRAINS TO FOLK FOOD CLASSICS – WATCH HOW WE BUBBLE AND RISE!

The idea of cakes and bakes as rituals is nothing new; they have long marked transformative moments in our lives, from birthdays to weddings to solstice celebrations. Here, I shift the focus to the ingredients themselves – the plants that infuse these recipes with power and meaning. These recipes act as manifestation rituals, with rising doughs or batters symbolizing growth and transformation.

For me, cooking and baking aren't just acts of nourishment – they're ways of connecting with the land, the seasons, and those I care about. The plants in these recipes can often be foraged, grounding us in the rhythms of nature, but accessibility is key. Whether using fresh, dried or store-bought varieties, these recipes are designed for everyone, wherever they live. Foraging (see page 27) adds a ceremonial layer to the process, but dried herbs can be just as powerful, keeping the magic alive year-round. (See page 202 for information on sourcing dried ingredients.)

In this chapter, I explore the folklore, histories and personal stories tied to seven of my favourite plants: sweet woodruff, heartsease, gorse, elderflower, sunflower, lavender and red clover. This list, however, is not exhaustive. What works for one might not for another. By taking the time to listen and using your own curiosity to lead, you can find what works best for you. As you bake, you'll be weaving your own narrative, grounded in the magic of ingredients that have connected humans to the earth for centuries.

SWEET WOODRUFF HOKKAIDO MILK BUNS

FOR VICTORY

This recipe is based on a traditional Hokkaido milk bread. The main flavour comes from the milk, which is infused with sweet woodruff. This has many magical properties, but the main way I use it is for 'victory'. With its delicate leaves and sweet scent, it has long been associated with winning and triumph. It tastes like sweet hay on a summer's day and is without doubt my favourite herb. I've tried it in cakes, puddings, drinks – but my favourite way to enjoy it is in this sweet and milky loaf, which can be separated into 3 delicious buns. If you are using this recipe to aid you in a specific victory, you can write your intention on a bay leaf and place it in the loaf tin, under the dough, before cooking. As the bread rises, so too will your alignment with success!

MAKES ONE SMALL LOAF (3 BUNS)

280g (2 cups) strong white bread flour, plus 2 tbsp for the tangzhong
60ml (¼ cup) sweet woodruff infused milk (see below)
1 tsp instant yeast
50g (¼ cup) caster (superfine) sugar
½ tsp sea salt
60g (¼ cup) butter, at room temperature
A little maple syrup, to wash

INFUSE YOUR MILK WITH THE FLAVOUR OF SWEET WOODRUFF BY ADDING A SMALL HANDFUL OF THE DRIED HERB TO A 200ML (7FL OZ) JAR OR BOTTLE OF MILK AND LETTING IT STEEP FOR AT LEAST A FEW HOURS – IDEALLY OVERNIGHT (I LIKE TO LEAVE MINE IN THE MOONLIGHT WHERE POSSIBLE!).

In a small saucepan over medium heat, combine the 2 tablespoons flour with 120ml (½ cup) water. Stir continuously for 4–5 minutes or until it forms a thick paste. Allow to cool to room temperature. This is your tangzhong.

Heat the milk to a lukewarm temperature and add the yeast and sugar. Leave for 5–10 minutes to develop into a frothy consistency.

Mix the tangzhong and yeast mixture into the flour and salt. Mix and knead for 10 minutes, working in the butter, bit by bit, as you knead. The dough may become sticky, but keep kneading until all the butter is worked in.

Cover the dough with a damp cloth or plastic wrap and let it rest until it doubles in size (around 2 hours). Meanwhile, grease and line a 900-g (2-lb) loaf tin with baking parchment. Toward the end of the proving time, preheat the oven to 180°C/350°F/Gas 4.

Once risen, knock the dough back (give it a punch) and knead slightly. Divide the dough into three equal portions. Roll each portion into a roughly 15-cm (6-inch) square and fold the opposite corners into the centre. Starting at one pointed end, roll the dough tightly. Place each piece of rolled dough seam side down in the prepared loaf tin. Cover and rest again for 30 minutes. Bake uncovered for 25–30 minutes until risen and slightly browned on top. Remove the loaf from the pan and lightly brush the top with a little maple syrup using a pastry brush. Leave as a loaf or tear into 3 buns.

This bread is best enjoyed within 2–3 days. Keep at room temperature in an airtight container.

GROWING ON MOIST AND SHADY FOREST FLOORS, THIS PLANT IS OFTEN USED IN BELTANE/MAY DAY CELEBRATIONS AND SUMMER RITUALS SYMBOLIZING THE RENEWAL OF LIFE AND THE TRIUMPH OF LIGHT OVER DARKNESS. IT CAN BE DRIED FOR USE THROUGHOUT THE YEAR – BRINGING A BIT OF SPRING VICTORY INTO EVEN THE DARKEST DAYS.

BLUEBERRY AND HEARTSEASE CREAM BREAD AND BUTTER PUDDING

TO EASE HEARTACHE

Also known as love-lies-bleeding, love-in-idleness, love-in-vain and, my personal favourite, tittle-my-fancy, the common pansy or heartsease, has an enigmatic warmth and friendliness. Pansies grow wild in temperate regions of Europe and North America, blooming from early spring to summer. The Romans said that pansies flowered white until hit by Cupid's arrow, when they would turn purple. My mother would grow pansies in abundant hanging baskets – so for me, they will always evoke happy childhood memories and feelings of home. A balm for soothing pain of the heart – both physical and emotional – this is the perfect plant for love potions and mending broken hearts. This sweet and warming deep-purple dessert evokes the comfort of simple childhood puds and joyful memories to cradle the hurting heart.

SERVES 6

FOR YOUR HEARTSEASE AND BLUEBERRY CREAM:
200ml (generous ¾ cup) milk
500ml (2 cups) whipping cream
200g (7oz) fresh blueberries
4 tbsp dried heartsease
1 tbsp maple syrup

FOR THE PUDDING:
80g (2¾oz) sultanas (golden raisins)
A splash of brandy
60ml (¼ cup) maple syrup
12 slices of bread
6 tbsp unsalted butter, plus extra for greasing
200g (7oz) fresh blueberries

The day before you wish to bake your pudding, put the sultanas in a bowl and add the brandy and maple syrup. Cover and leave to soak overnight.

To make your heartsease and blueberry cream simply bring all the ingredients to a gentle simmer in a saucepan for 2 minutes. Allow to cool, then strain, crushing as much juice from the blueberries as possible. Stir and set aside.

Preheat your oven to 180°C/350°F/Gas 4 and grease a 23 x 33cm (9 x 13 inch) baking tin with butter. Butter the bread slices on both sides and sit them in the pan, overlapping each other.

Sprinkle over the soaked sultanas and blueberries and pour the cream on top. Bake for 25 minutes until the top is golden.

Enjoy in a cozy setting with friends or watching a movie – a simple act of self-care for those who might need some love and tenderness.

IN MANY FOLK AND MAGICAL TRADITIONS, THE GATHERING OF THE PLANTS AND HERBS SEEMS TO BE INTEGRAL TO THE PROCESS OF THE RECIPE. YOU'LL OFTEN SEE IT NOTED IN THE 'COMMONPLACE BOOKS' TO 'PICK THIS PLANT ON MIDSUMMER' OR 'GATHER WHEN THE MOON IS FULL'. THIS CAN SEEM ODDLY SPECIFIC, BUT THE POTENCY OF A PLANT CAN BE AFFECTED BY THE TIME OF YEAR AND THE MOONLIGHT. PLANTS OFTEN RELEASE THEIR POLLEN AT NIGHT, SO IT CAN BE A GREAT TIME TO FORAGE.

GORSE FLOWER PASTEL DE NATA

FOR ENDURING LOVE

Gorse flowers hold a special place in my heart. They remind me of one of my favourite places – the mystical moors of Dartmoor in the beautiful English county of Devon. Dartmoor has an ancient, untamed beauty, and the golden blossoms of gorse, which light up the wild landscape amongst the heather and rocky tors, are its constant companion. In Celtic mythology, gorse was believed to protect against evil spirits and was often planted around homes as a shield. Druids considered it sacred, using its flowers in Beltane fires to celebrate fertility and the return of summer. Native to Western Europe and parts of North Africa, and often found in heathlands, coastal areas and open fields, the flowers are most abundant in late winter and early spring. These pastel de natas capture the power of the gorse – a reminder of Dartmoor's timeless spirit, a symbol of resilience and enduring love.

MAKES 12

1 tbsp fresh gorse petals, finely chopped, plus extra petals to garnish
400ml (14fl oz) coconut milk
30g (1oz) fresh gorse flowers, plus extra for garnishing (or 3g dried)
100g (½ cup) caster (superfine) sugar
2 tbsp cornflour (cornstarch)
1 tsp vanilla extract
1 tbsp lemon juice
¼ tsp ground turmeric
Butter, for greasing
Plain (all-purpose) flour, for dusting
500g (1lb 2oz) block of puff pastry

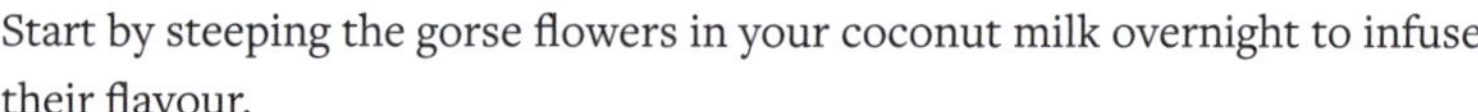

Start by steeping the gorse flowers in your coconut milk overnight to infuse their flavour.

The next day, strain the milk, but save a few petals to stir into the custard mixture.

In a saucepan, combine the infused coconut milk, sugar, cornflour, vanilla extract, lemon juice, and a pinch of turmeric for colour. Whisk over medium heat until the mixture thickens into a smooth custard, then stir in the finely chopped fresh gorse petals for added texture.

Preheat the oven to 180°C/350°F/Gas 4 and grease a 12-hole muffin tin with butter.

On a lightly dusted surface, roll out the puff pastry and, using a 9-cm (3½ -inch) round cookie cutter, stamp out 12 circles, and press them into the holes of the greased muffin tin. Fill each pastry shell with the gorse-infused custard. Bake for about 20–25 minutes, until the pastry is golden and the custard slightly set.

Garnish with extra gorse petals before serving for an extra touch of botanical magic. These are best enjoyed on the day of baking, but they will keep for 3–4 days in an airtight container in the fridge. Share with those you love as each one represents love's enduring kiss.

FOLKLORE DECLARES THAT YOU SHOULD ONLY KISS YOUR LOVED ONES WHEN THE GORSE IS IN BLOOM – WHAT IS DELIGHTFUL ABOUT THIS DECREE IS THAT THESE BRIGHT YELLOW FLOWERS, WITH THEIR COCONUT-SCENTED SWEETNESS, THRIVE YEAR-ROUND, BRINGING WARMTH TO EVEN THE HARSHEST SEASONS. THIS ETERNAL BLOOM SYMBOLIZES ENDURING LOVE AND PERSEVERANCE.

LEMON, ELDERFLOWER AND POPPYSEED POPPET DRIZZLE SWIRL BUNS

FOR EASING WORRIES IN YOUR SLEEP

The elder tree holds a cherished place in my memory, its canopy providing a protective haven for one of my childhood dens. Elderflowers have long been associated with warding off evil and symbolize transformation and the cycles of life. Poppies – tied deeply to sleep, dreams and protection in folklore – carry powerful symbolism. Poppy seeds, used in dream pillows or charms, are believed to encourage restful sleep and represent transformation, life and rebirth. This recipe weaves together elderflower and poppy magic, drawing on their folkloric connections to protection and dream magic. These buns will bring sweet dreams, answering your questions or easing your worries.

MAKES 12

FOR THE DOUGH:
30g (1oz) poppy seeds
500g (3¾ cups) plain (all-purpose) flour
7g (¼oz) instant yeast
75g (6 tbsp) sugar
½ tsp sea salt
250ml (1 cup) milk
75g (5 tbsp) butter, melted, plus extra for greasing
Finely grated zest of 1 lemon

FOR THE FILLING:
100g (½ cup less 1 tbsp) butter, softened
50g (¼ cup) sugar
Finely grated zest of 1 lemon
2 tbsp elderflower cordial

FOR THE ELDERFLOWER LEMON DRIZZLE:
50ml (3½ tbsp) elderflower cordial
Juice of 1 lemon
100g (¾ cup) icing (powdered) sugar

A POPPET IS A SMALL DOLL OR FIGURE, OFTEN MADE OF CLOTH OR WAX, USED IN FOLK MAGIC OR WITCHCRAFT. POPPETS ARE OFTEN FILLED WITH HERBS, PERSONAL ITEMS OR SYMBOLS RELATED TO THE INTENTION. THEIR USE IS ROOTED IN SYMPATHETIC MAGIC, WHERE ACTIONS PERFORMED ON THE POPPET ARE BELIEVED TO AFFECT THE PERSON IT SYMBOLIZES.

The night before making the buns, place your poppy seeds in a small bag or vial – this is your poppet. Before bed, whisper your troubles or questions to the poppyseed poppet, and place it under your pillow as you sleep, treating it gently as it represents you. It will seek answers or dispel fears in the dream realm.

The next day, start by making the dough. In a large bowl, combine the flour, yeast, sugar and salt. Warm the milk in a saucepan, stirring in the melted butter and lemon zest. Let this cool slightly so as not to kill the yeast. Pour this mixture into the dry ingredients, mixing until a soft dough forms. Add the poppy seeds from your poppet and knead for 8–10 minutes, until smooth and elastic. Cover the dough with a damp cloth and let it rise for 1–1½ hours in a warm place, until doubled in size.

While the dough rises, prepare the filling. In a bowl, mix the softened butter, sugar, lemon zest, and elderflower cordial until creamy. Grease a 23 x 33-cm (9 x 13-inch) baking tin with butter.

Once the dough has risen, punch it down, then roll it into a rectangle measuring roughly 40 x 30cm (16 x 12 inches) on a lightly floured surface. Spread the filling evenly over the dough. Roll the dough up tightly from the shorter end, then slice the log into 12 pieces. Arrange the buns, cut-sides up, in the greased tin. Cover the buns and let them rise for another 30–45 minutes.

Toward the end of the proving time, preheat your oven to 180°C/350°F/ Gas 4. Bake the buns for 20–25 minutes until golden brown.

While baking, make the drizzle by whisking together the elderflower cordial, lemon juice and icing sugar. Once the buns have cooled slightly, drizzle the glaze over them, allowing it to soak in. These buns will keep for 2–3 days in an airtight container at room temperature or 5–6 days in an airtight container in the fridge.

SUNFLOWER SEED BUTTER LOAF

TO BRING SOMEONE HOME SAFELY

In folklore, sunflowers represent devotion and creativity, and are often used in rituals for positivity and happiness. Their sun-like appearance is believed to attract loyalty, light and joy. I have a tradition with a friend who brings me flowers whenever he picks me up from the airport after going on my travels – where possible he always makes sure to get me sunflowers. For me they will always evoke feelings of pure joy and feeling 'home'. This is an especially witchy bake because of the colour – the chlorophyl in sunflower seeds reacts with baking powder in this recipe transforming the sponge into a mystical green hue. I recommend making this loaf to welcome someone home whom you have missed, or add a bay leaf with a sigil of someone's name to ensure a safe and harmonious journey home.

SERVES 6–8

1 tsp ground cinnamon (plus 1 tsp for the ritual)
250g (1 cup) sunflower seed butter
120ml (½ cup) almond milk
60ml (¼ cup) maple syrup
1 tsp vanilla extract
180g (1 1/3 cups) plain (all-purpose) flour
1 tsp baking powder
½ tsp bicarbonate of soda (baking soda)
¼ tsp sea salt
60g (heaped ½ cup) oats

Before you begin, place one of your teaspoons of cinnamon into your palm and blow it into the direction of the person you are calling home – no matter where they are in the world. You may want to use a compass for this – or you can blow it onto a photograph of them if you are not sure of the direction.

Preheat your oven to 180°C/350°F/Gas 4 and line a 900-g (2-lb) loaf pan with baking parchment.

In a large bowl, whisk together the sunflower seed butter, almond milk, maple syrup and vanilla extract until smooth.

In a separate bowl, stir together the flour, baking powder, bicarbonate of soda, remaining cinnamon and salt. Gradually add the dry ingredients to the wet mixture, stirring until just combined – be careful not to overmix. Gently stir in your oats to sow in your intention – whether that be for joy, creativity or devotion.

Pour the batter into the prepared loaf pan and smooth the top with a spatula. Bake for 30–35 minutes, or until a toothpick inserted into the centre comes out clean. Let the loaf cool in the pan for about 10 minutes, then transfer it to a wire rack to cool completely. Once cooled, slice and serve as is, or spread with extra seed butter for added richness.

IN GREEK MYTHOLOGY, THE SUNFLOWER IS LINKED TO THE STORY OF APOLLO AND THE NYMPH CLYTIE. IN LOVE WITH APOLLO, A GOD ASSOCIATED WITH THE SUN, CLYTIE WATCHED HIM CROSS THE SKY DAILY. DESPITE HER DEVOTION, APOLLO SPURNED HER, CAUSING HER TO WITHER AWAY, EVENTUALLY TRANSFORMING INTO A SUNFLOWER. THIS MYTH SYMBOLIZES UNREQUITED LOVE AND LOYALTY, WITH SUNFLOWERS ETERNALLY TURNING TOWARD THE SUN, ECHOING CLYTIE'S LONGING FOR APOLLO.

PANDAN AND LAVENDER BATTENBERG

FOR CALM AND PROTECTION

In 2022, I came home to my boat after a night away to find it severely vandalized. For a long while after, my home was a place that induced fear and panic. One way I reclaimed my space was by burning lavender to cleanse the negativity and anxiety in the air. Lavender has long been associated with purity, calm, and protection. In medieval times, lavender was burned to purify homes and ward off plague. Medicinally, lavender is known for its soothing properties, often used to relieve stress, anxiety and insomnia. Lavender's fragrant aroma is believed to promote clarity, healing and emotional balance, making it a versatile herb in both magical and medicinal practices. For me, a Battenberg is the most quintessentially twee British cake – reminiscent of summer fetes and afternoon tea – so there is no better cake to calm the nerves! As you prepare it, focus on the calming properties of the lavender as well as the peace that a simple act of mindful baking can bring.

SERVES 6-8

FOR THE PANDAN SPONGE:
120g (scant 1 cup) plain (all-purpose) flour
100g (½ cup) caster (superfine) sugar
1 tsp baking powder
½ tsp bicarbonate of soda (baking soda)
¼ tsp sea salt
120ml (½ cup) almond milk
60ml (¼ cup) vegetable oil
2 tsp pandan extract (or pandan paste)

FOR THE LAVENDER SPONGE:
120g (scant 1 cup) flour
100g (½ cup) caster (superfine) sugar
1 tsp baking powder
½ tsp bicarbonate of soda (baking soda)
¼ tsp sea salt
120ml (½ cup) almond milk
60ml (¼ cup) vegetable oil
1 tbsp dried lavender

FOR THE MARZIPAN AND GLAZE:
200g (7oz) marzipan
Icing (powdered) sugar, for dusting
Apricot jam, for glazing

Preheat your oven to 180°C/350°F/Gas 4 and grease and line two 20-cm (8-inch) loaf pans.

For the pandan sponge, mix together the flour, sugar, baking powder, bicarbonate of soda, and salt. In a separate bowl, whisk the almond milk, oil and pandan extract. Combine the wet and dry ingredients, being careful not to overmix, then pour the batter into one of the prepared loaf pans.

For the lavender sponge, repeat the same process, substituting the dried lavender for pandan extract. Pour the batter into the second pan.

Bake both sponges for 25–30 minutes, until a toothpick inserted comes out clean. Remove the cakes from the pans and let them cool completely before trimming the edges and cutting each cake in half lengthwise. Trim the sponge so you are left with four square strips, two pandan, two lavender.

Arrange the strips in a checkerboard pattern by placing one pandan strip next to one lavender strip, then alternating the colours on top. Brush each side with apricot jam to stick them together as you assemble.

Dust your work surface with a little icing sugar and roll out the marzipan into a 20 x 15-cm (8 x 6-inch) rectangle that is about 3mm (1/8 inch) thick. Brush all sides of the cake with apricot jam, then place it at one edge of the marzipan sheet. Roll it up tightly, trimming any excess and pressing firmly to seal. Lightly dust with icing sugar before serving. Enjoy with a calming cup of tea.

RED CLOVER AND NUTMEG LUCKY COOKIES

FOR LUCK

Being lucky enough to spend much of my childhood with access to the countryside, many of my days were filled with making daisy chains, climbing trees, getting piskie-led in the woods – and spending hours searching for that elusive four-leafed clover in the grass fields. Red clover has long been associated with luck and protection in folklore. Traditionally, finding a four-leaf clover was believed to bring good fortune and guard against evil spirits. In Celtic mythology, clover symbolized abundance and was often used in rituals to attract wealth and prosperity. Historically, red clover was also valued for its medicinal properties, and used to treat respiratory issues, skin ailments, and to purify the blood. I like to make these cookies right before something important when I need a boost – carry one with you to enjoy after a job interview, for example.

MAKES 6 COOKIES

115g (½ cup) butter
100g (½ cup) brown sugar, plus extra to sprinkle
100g (½ cup) caster (superfine) sugar
30ml (2 tbsp) milk
1 tsp vanilla extract
190g (1 ⅓ cup) plain (all-purpose) flour
1 tbsp dried red clover, finely ground
1 tsp ground nutmeg
½ tsp ground allspice
½ tsp bicarbonate of soda (baking soda)
¼ tsp sea salt

Preheat your oven to 180°C/350°F/Gas 4 and line a baking sheet with baking parchment.

In a large bowl, cream together the butter, brown sugar and caster sugar until light and fluffy. Stir in the milk and vanilla extract.

In a separate bowl, whisk together the flour, ground clover, nutmeg, allspice, bicarbonate of soda and salt. Gradually combine the dry ingredients with the wet mixture until smooth.

Roll the dough into small balls, about 1 tablespoon each, and place them on the prepared baking sheet. Gently flatten each ball. Bake for 10–12 minutes until the edges turn golden. Let the cookies cool on the baking sheet for a few minutes, then transfer to a wire rack to cool completely.

Sprinkle with brown sugar and enjoy while still warm to invite luck into your life!

IN CELTIC FOLKLORE, IT'S IMPORTANT TO SEEK PERMISSION FROM PISKIES AND FAIRIES BEFORE GATHERING WILDFLOWERS, DEMONSTRATING RESPECT FOR NATURE. BEING 'PISKIE-LED' REFERS TO GETTING LOST DUE TO THE MISCHIEVOUS INFLUENCE OF THESE PLAYFUL BEINGS. IN IRELAND AND ICELAND, ROADS AND LANDMARKS ARE SOMETIMES INTENTIONALLY BUILT TO AVOID FAIRY HAUNTS, SHOWING REVERENCE FOR THESE MYSTICAL CREATURES. DISREGARDING SUCH CUSTOMS IS BELIEVED TO BRING MISFORTUNE, AS FAIRIES ARE KNOWN FOR THEIR MISCHIEF AND VENGEANCE. WHETHER SUPERSTITION OR NOT, IT'S OFTEN WISER TO STAY ON THEIR GOOD SIDE.

CEREMONIAL RECIPES

FEASTS FOR THE WHEEL OF THE YEAR

Most of us are familiar with a few of the 'Pagan' festivals of the year, or at least their Christian and secular counterparts. Observing these celebrations does not need to stem from a deeply religious or spiritual connection – providing we stay mindful and respectful toward the cultures from which they originated. Creating ceremony around the turning of the Wheel of the Year can hold deeper significance while remaining ultimately un-dogmatic.

Marking these sacred days connects us to the passing of the seasons, nostalgia, tradition, ancestral wisdom and time well spent. Most of these festivals are born from Celtic pagan traditions, however the seasonal changes they represent are the same for many places around the world.

Many of these ceremonies recognize the symbiotic relationship with nature that we all crave as we become increasingly disconnected from the natural world. The recipes in this section follow the Wheel of the Year (below), so you too can celebrate the changing seasons. By embracing them, we can enhance our lives, express gratitude for its simple beauty, and ultimately move in harmony with nature's endless wheel. I've experienced the transformative power of these festivals first hand, hosting gatherings and rituals that celebrate the magic inherent throughout the year.

IMBOLC

FEBRUARY 1ST

A CELEBRATION OF RENEWAL

As winter's hold begins to loosen, Imbolc emerges as a quiet celebration of hope and renewal. Imbolc is a Celtic festival of light and life, a bridge between winter and spring, a time when the earth is still sleeping, but full of potential.

Candles are lit to illuminate the still-dark evenings, to honour the sun's return and to welcome Brigid, the Celtic goddess of poetry, healing and crafts, whose feast day coincides with Imbolc. Her presence is felt in the act of creating something new in anticipation of the year's unfolding. This is a time for reflection, setting intentions and laying the groundwork for future growth.

The festival's name, derived from the Gaelic oimelc, meaning 'ewe's milk', connects Imbolc to fertility and sustenance. Early spring greens and nettles begin to emerge, their resilience and vitality offering a glimpse of the bounty to come. These hardy plants remind us to tread lightly and appreciate the tender growth that is yet fragile but full of promise.

In the stillness of the season, other traditions around the world echo the themes of Imbolc. In the Lunar New Year celebrated across East Asia, symbolic foods and rituals usher in prosperity and fresh beginnings. In Nordic cultures, candle festivals herald the sun's growing strength, while Setsubun in Japan involves casting out negativity to welcome renewal.

Imbolc invites us to pause and notice the earth's subtle transformations. It's a time to light the hearth, gather loved ones, and honour the balance of rest and readiness. Through each act of intention – whether crafting, feasting or planting seeds – we prepare for the flourishing days of spring.

CREAMED THREE-CORNERED LEEK

PAYING HOMAGE TO THE ORIGINS OF IMBOLC

Three-cornered leek, a wild green that emerges in early spring, invites us to pause and consider the first signs of life pushing through the still, cold earth. Growing in damp, shaded areas, three-cornered leek is commonly found in woodlands and riverbanks, and is native to the Mediterranean but has since spread to various parts of Europe, the UK and parts of North America. By February 1st, in temperate regions, you should begin to see the first shoots and leaves. Although the plant's flowers, which are a key identifying feature, generally bloom in March, its distinctive triangular hollow stalk and garlic-like smell make its greens relatively easy to identify, even before the flowers come in. The creamy nature of this dish represents the origins of Imbolc (even if your cream is not the traditional dairy – it's all about the symbolism!). It's perfect for celebrating the arrival of lightm the blessing of Brigid and Spring's return. Your three-cornered leek should be gathered with mindful intention – notice how the earth is still sleeping, alive only with potential.

SERVES 4 (AS A SIDE DISH)

1 tbsp olive oil
1 garlic clove, minced
a generous handful of three-cornered leek, finely chopped (you can substitute three-cornered leek for spring onions (scallions) if you struggle to find it in the wild!)
300ml (1¼ cups) cream
1 tsp finely grated lemon zest
Sea salt and black pepper
A pinch of nutmeg

Start by heating the olive oil in a large skillet over medium heat. Add the minced garlic and sauté for a minute, ensuring it doesn't burn. Add your chopped three-cornered leek and sauté for another minute.

Lower the heat and pour in the cream, stirring well to combine. Add the lemon zest, and season with salt, pepper and a pinch of nutmeg. Let the mixture simmer for a few minutes, allowing the flavours to meld and the sauce to thicken slightly.

Remove from the heat, adjust the seasoning if needed, and serve warm as part of a feast shared with friends, by candlelight.

IMBOLC IS ASSOCIATED WITH WEAVING AND CRAFT. IT IS TRADITIONAL TO MAKE A ST BRIGID'S CROSS AND DECORATE THE HOME WITH IT. THESE ARE USUALLY MADE FROM RUSHES, REEDS OR STRAW. TRY CRAFTING A ST BRIGID'S CROSS TOGETHER AFTER YOUR FEAST – OR GET TOGETHER TO HOLD A SEWING/KNITTING CIRCLE.

NETTLE LEAF SPANAKOPITA PIE

SWEEPING AWAY NEGATIVITY

Nettles are associated with protection, healing and purification, making them fitting symbols for warding off negativity and starting the new year afresh. As you forage for nettles, gather bare twigs to craft a simple besom (broomstick) for your kitchen. The besom will not only cleanse your space but also represents the cleansing of your life and honours the craftsmanship of St Brigid. The act of foraging the nettle and making your besom is as much a part of the ritual as the cooking and eating!

SERVES 4–6

200g (7oz) nettle leaves
200g (7oz) spinach, finely chopped
½ tsp salt
175g (6oz) Greek-style cheese of choice, crumbled
120g (½ cup) yogurt
2 tbsp finely chopped mint
2 tbsp finely chopped parsley
1 tbsp finely chopped dill
½ tsp lemon zest
½ tbsp lemon juice
2 garlic cloves, finely chopped
½ tsp freshly grated nutmeg
¼ tsp black pepper
¼ tsp sea salt
1 small apple, peeled and finely diced
60g (2oz) walnuts, roughly chopped
10 sheets filo (phyllo) pastry
120g (½ cup) butter, melted
1 tsp black sesame seeds
Maple syrup or honey, to serve

YOU WILL ALSO NEED:
Gathered twigs and nettles
Twine

Start by making your besom: bind gathered twigs and some fresh nettles with twine to form a small broom. Use it to sweep your work area, symbolically clearing out negativity to create space for renewal and intention. This is a tradition you can continue for each ritual recipe you make throughout the year.

Preheat the oven to 180°C/350°F/Gas 4 and line a 23 x 33 x 7-cm (9 x 13 x 3-inch) baking tin with baking parchment.

Start the recipe by steaming your nettle leaves in a steamer basket over a pan of simmering water for 3–5 minutes until wilted and tender. This will neutralize the sting. Put them in a bowl of iced water to cool and drain them before handling.

Chop the nettles and raw spinach roughly, toss them with a generous pinch of salt and let them sit for about 10 minutes in a colander to sweat. Once wilted, use a clean tea towel to wring out the excess water.

In a large bowl, combine the nettles and spinach with the crumbled cheese, yogurt, fresh herbs, lemon zest and juice, garlic, nutmeg, pepper, salt, diced apple and walnuts. Mix well, focusing on your intentions for protection and renewal as you stir.

To assemble the pie, layer five sheets of filo pastry into your prepared baking tin, brushing each sheet with melted butter as you go. Spread the filling evenly over the pastry. Add five more sheets of pastry, once again buttering between each sheet. Finish the final pastry layer with a brush of butter and sprinkle of black sesame seeds on top, then bake for 25 minutes or until golden.

Serve whilst still hot and crisp, drizzled with maple syrup or honey. Enjoy with friends whilst contemplating the purification and protection you've welcomed into your space.

CARAWAY SEED IMBOLC FAIRINGS

A NEW YEAR'S INTENTION SPELL

Fairings, traditionally spiced Cornish biscuits, have long been associated with festive gatherings and small celebratory gifts, particularly in the UK. These crunchy treats date back to the 19th century and were often sold at fairs, hence the name. The addition of caraway seeds gives these fairings a link to Imbolc, as it's a traditional time to eat them. Seeds are symbolic of new beginnings, fertility and protection, making them the perfect ingredient for this recipe which invites you to create an intentional start to the year.

MAKES 8 SMALL FAIRINGS

150g (1 cup plus 2 tbsp) plain (all-purpose) flour
1 tsp baking powder
1 tsp ground ginger
1 tsp ground cinnamon
½ tsp ground nutmeg
A pinch of sea salt
1 tbsp caraway seeds
75g (5 tbsp) butter
50g (¼ cup) light brown sugar
1 tbsp golden syrup (light corn syrup)

YOU WILL ALSO NEED:
A candle
A sheet of paper and a pen

Begin by lighting the candle to open the circle. As the flame flickers, take out the sheet of paper and handwrite eight personal intentions you would like to see come to fruition this year.

Preheat the oven to at 180°C/350°F/Gas 4 and line a baking sheet with baking parchment.

In a large bowl, sift together the flour, baking powder, ginger, cinnamon, nutmeg and a pinch of salt. Stir in the caraway seeds, allowing their symbolism of new beginnings to blend with the other ingredients.

In a pan, melt the butter, brown sugar and golden syrup over low heat until smooth. Remove from the heat and pour the mixture into the dry ingredients. Stir gently with a wooden spoon. Add 1 tablespoon water slowly to bring the dough together. Shape the dough into eight equal-sized balls and place them on the prepared baking sheet. Flatten each ball slightly with the back of a spoon, imprinting your energy into every biscuit.

Bake the fairings in the preheated oven for 10–12 minutes, or until golden brown. While the fairings bake, reflect on the light and warmth of the candle.

Once cooled, place the fairings in a cookie tin or jar. Over the next 4 days, eat two fairings a day with warm tea or moon milk (see page 150 onwards). As you savour each biscuit, focus on one specific goal, visualizing it clearly and committing to it. After finishing the fairings, place your handwritten goals into an envelope and tuck it inside the tin or jar. Hide the container somewhere in your home, to be reopened on winter solstice as a reminder of the intentions you set at Imbolc.

THE MODERN CALENDAR PUSHES US TO LEAP INTO PRODUCTIVITY ON NEW YEAR'S DAY, LEADING TO BURNOUT BY MID-JANUARY. IMBOLC HOWEVER, REMINDS US THAT JANUARY CAN INSTEAD BE A PERIOD FOR RESTING, STILLNESS AND CONTEMPLATION. IT TEACHES US NOT TO RUSH INTO ACTION WHILE THE EARTH IS STILL SLEEPING, BUT TO PAUSE, REFLECT AND CONSIDER OUR INTENTIONS MORE CAREFULLY.

SPRING EQUINOX

AROUND MARCH 21ST

BALANCE AND NEW BEGINNINGS

Around March 20th or 21st in the Northern Hemisphere, the Spring Equinox marks a moment of perfect balance between day and night. The word equinox comes from the Latin *'aequus'* (equal) and *'nox'* (night), symbolizing equal lengths of daylight and darkness – both in nature and within us.

Historically, the equinox was a significant time for agricultural societies, marking the halfway point between winter and summer, when it was time to begin preparing for the fertile season ahead. The Spring Equinox was seen as a moment for both reflection and action – an invitation to honour the balance of light and dark, just as the day and night were equally balanced. In many traditions, this time was for clearing away the old and making space for new opportunities. Spring cleaning and home purification rituals were common, symbolizing the renewal of both the external world and the inner self.

Today, the Spring Equinox continues to inspire celebrations of new beginnings, a time when people might plant seeds, both in the earth and in their lives, and set intentions for the months ahead. As the earth begins to wake from its winter slumber, it offers us a chance to do the same, aligning with nature's rhythms to foster growth, transformation and balance. This is a time to reflect on the potential within, as the world around us bursts into bloom, inviting us to embrace the season of rebirth and possibility.

STORE CUPBOARD SODA BREAD

A SPRING CLEANSING RITUAL

The act of 'spring cleaning' is traditional for this time of year – clearing out the old to bring in the new. This can be done in a very practical sense, but it also represents a clear out of one's life.

STORE CUPBOARD CLEARING RITUAL

Gather your tools: Before you begin, collect a notebook, a pen, a small bowl of Four Thieves' Vinegar (see page 38) and a soft cloth.

Create a sacred space: Set the mood with soft lighting or candles. Take a few deep breaths to centre yourself.

Cleanse the space: Clear any clutter. Wipe down shelves with a natural cleaner or a sage bundle to refresh the energy.

Assess your supplies: Mindfully take stock of what you have, noting each item with gratitude for its purpose.

Let go of the old: Remove expired or unwanted items, releasing anything that no longer serves your kitchen's needs.

Restock with purpose: Make a list of what to buy. Choose items that align with your seasonal goals: energy, comfort, health.

Seal with gratitude: Place a small token (a crystal, leaf or symbol) in the cupboard as a reminder of abundance. Give thanks for all that you've been given and all that is yet to come.

Assemble your bread ingredients: Most likely during your clear out, you will have come across odds and ends of herbs, spices, dried fruit, nuts and seeds – choose which of these you would like to add into your bread to complete the ritual.

SERVES 4–6

- **1 tbsp apple cider vinegar**
- **240ml (1 cup) milk**
- **240g (1¾ cups) spelt flour**
- **1 tbsp sugar**
- **½ tsp baking powder**
- **1 tsp bicarbonate of soda (baking soda)**
- **½ tsp sea salt**
- **60g (4 tbsp) butter, softened, plus extra for greasing and to serve**
- **Herbs and spices of your choosing, to taste**
- **40g (1½oz) dried fruit, chopped**
- **30g (1oz) seeds and nuts of your choice, plus a few extra seeds for the top**

Preheat the oven to 200°C/400°F/Gas 6 and grease a 20-cm (8-inch) round cake tin with butter.

Pour the apple cider vinegar into the milk and let it sit for 5 minutes to curdle.

Combine the flour, sugar, baking powder, bicarbonate of soda and salt in a large bowl. Add the butter and work it into the dry ingredients with your fingertips, as you would a crumble. Add the vinegar and milk mixture and bring together into a dough, then work in your chosen herbs, dried fruit, nuts and seeds. Plop the dough into the prepared tin and sprinkle more seeds on top. Cut a cross into it to let the fairies out and bake in the preheated oven for 25 minutes until golden.

While the bread bakes, write down three things you would like to let go of from your life and three things you would like to invite in. Enjoy your bread while still warm with cold butter, ruminating on the changes you would like to attract into your life. Place the note into your cupboard to remind you of your intentions each time you cook.

WILD GARLIC ANCIENT GRAIN HUSBAND BLINDERS

INVITING PROTECTION IN AS WE REAWAKEN

All garlic is associated with protection and banishing negative energy, but wild garlic has a specific link to reawakening and renewal, so it feels especially pertinent that it usually emerges around the Spring Equinox. Found growing in damp, shaded woodlands and along riverbanks across Europe and parts of North America, throughout spring (March to May), it thrives in moist, well-drained soil and can often be identified by its broad, lance-shaped leaves and strong garlic scent. It's best to harvest it before the plant flowers, as the flavour is most vibrant at this time. It's one of the first notable foraging plants that appears in the year and so, too, the gathering can help us come out of our own hibernations. This peppery and chewy pasta dish connects to heirloom cooking without tools and embraces the power of wild garlic to bring protection and sustenance after a long winter.

SERVES 4

500g (1lb 2oz) wild garlic, fresh and cleaned (or 30g/1oz dried)
250g (1 cup) double (heavy) cream
A pinch of freshly grated nutmeg
1 tbsp olive oil, plus a splash for the pasta water
200g (7oz) cherry tomatoes, sliced in half
100g (3½oz) cheese of your choice, grated
50g (1¾oz) pine nuts
Sea salt and black pepper

FOR THE HUSBAND BLINDERS PASTA:
360g (2¾ cups) khorasan flour
3 tbsp apple cider vinegar
1 tsp sea salt

To make the pasta, put the flour, vinegar and salt in a bowl with 250ml (1 cup) water and mix to form a stiff dough. Knead for 7–8 minutes until smooth and elastic. Consider the process of kneading the pasta dough as an opportunity for personal renewal. As you knead the dough, focus on reawakening your own energy after the dormant winter months. With each fold and press of the dough, visualize yourself shedding the last remnants of winter and stepping into the freshness of spring. Cover the dough and let it rest overnight in the fridge.

For the creamed wild garlic, blanch the garlic in boiling water for 2 minutes, then transfer it to an ice bath for 1 minute. Drain, then squeeze out the excess water and finely chop. Combine with the cream, a pinch of salt, pepper and nutmeg, then set aside.

On a floured surface, roll hazelnut-sized pieces of dough into sausages with pinched ends to form 'husband blinders', a rustic Italian pasta so tasty it is said to dazzle men. Boil them in salted, oiled water for 3–4 minutes until tender, in batches if needed, to prevent sticking. Drain and set aside.

In a pan, heat the oil and lightly sear the sliced tomatoes until they gain colour. Remove the tomatoes from the pan, then gently heat the pasta and creamed wild garlic, taking care not to boil. Plate the pasta and arrange the tomatoes on top, then sprinkle with cheese and pine nuts and season with salt and pepper. Enjoy this dish whilst inviting in protection and the energy to bring you out of your winter hibernation and into spring.

KHORASAN FLOUR, ALSO KNOWN AS 'KAMUT', IS AN ANCIENT GRAIN WHICH IS MUCH HIGHER IN AMINO ACIDS, FIBRE AND PROTEIN THAN TRADITIONAL WHEAT FLOUR. NOT ONLY DOES IT HAVE THIS BENEFICIAL NUTRITIONAL PROFILE, IT ALSO HAS A DEEP AND DELICIOUS NUTTY FLAVOUR.

MAGNOLIA AND HIBISCUS POACHED PEAR PANNA COTTA

HONOURING BALANCE

Magnolia flowers typically bloom in early spring, from March to May, and can be found in temperate areas across North America, Europe and Asia. Magnolia flowers hold a special place in both nature and folklore. In European witchcraft, magnolia's uses range from fostering love and harmony to providing spiritual protection. Its flowers are incorporated into rituals to promote balance, calm from emotional turbulence, and to ward off negative energy. The enchanting blend of soft grace and hardy durability makes it a powerful symbol of femininity, beauty and endurance. This dish represents the resilience of getting through winter and making it to spring. The pears, poached in wine and spices, remind us of winter flavours while the creamy floral panna cotta encapsulates the taste of spring – representing the balance of the meeting seasons, and also the balance within ourselves.

SERVES 4

FOR THE MAGNOLIA-INFUSED PANNA COTTA:

400ml (1¾ cups) double (heavy) cream
100ml (scant ½ cup) milk
6 fresh magnolia petals, washed, plus more for decoration
50g (¼ cup) caster (superfine) sugar
1 tsp vanilla extract
1½ tsp agar-agar powder

FOR THE HIBISCUS-POACHED PEARS:

350ml (1½ cups) red wine
50g (¼ cup) sugar
2 tbsp dried hibiscus flowers (or 2 hibiscus tea bags)
1 cinnamon stick
1 star anise
2 small ripe pears, peeled, cored and halved

YOU WILL ALSO NEED:

4 silicone moulds, about 150ml (5fl oz) each

Start by making the magnolia-infused panna cotta. Combine the cream and milk in a saucepan, then add the magnolia petals, taking a moment to hold each petal in your hands before placing it into the cream. As you hold the petal, gently close your eyes and silently express gratitude for the resilience that comes with the changing seasons, acknowledging the energy of spring's return. Heat gently until it steams (don't let it boil). Remove from the heat, cover and steep overnight in the fridge.

The next day, poach the pears. Combine the red wine, sugar, dried hibiscus, cinnamon and star anise in a saucepan. Simmer until the sugar dissolves, then add the peeled, halved pears. Simmer for 20–30 minutes more, turning occasionally. Once tender, remove the pears and keep cooking to reduce the wine mixture to a syrupy consistency. Strain and set aside.

For each panna cotta, strain the magnolia petals from the cream, then heat the cream with the sugar and vanilla until the sugar dissolves. Dissolve the agar-agar in a splash of cold water, then add it to the cream and simmer for a few minutes. Pour into the silicone moulds and refrigerate for 3–4 hours until set.

To serve, unmould the panna cotta, place a poached pear beside it and drizzle with the hibiscus reduction. Garnish with fresh magnolia petals and enjoy as a celebration to welcome the vitality of spring into your life.

ONE OF THE OLDEST FLOWERING PLANTS, MAGNOLIAS PREDATE BEES AND WERE ORIGINALLY POLLINATED BY BEETLES, WHICH IS WHY THEIR PETALS ARE SO THICK AND DURABLE. IN FOLKLORE, MAGNOLIA FLOWERS ARE OFTEN ASSOCIATED WITH STRENGTH, DIGNITY AND PERSEVERANCE DUE TO THE TREE'S ABILITY TO THRIVE IN A RANGE OF ENVIRONMENTS.

BELTANE

MAY 1ST

FIRE AND FERTILITY

Beltane, celebrated on May 1st, is a festival of fire and fertility, marking the peak of spring and the approach of summer. This vibrant celebration is rich in folk traditions, especially in rural areas of the UK, where it has remained a national holiday (although not primarily recognized by its Pagan roots). The name 'Beltane' derives from the Celtic god Belenus, associated with the sun, fire and fertility. The festival celebrates the union of nature's masculine and feminine energies and invites us to connect with the Earth's creative force.

The sun looms high in the sky, bathing the fields in golden light while trees burst with verdant leaves. Maypoles are erected and ribbons sail in the wind as people dance, feast and revel. Morris dancers' bells jingle in the fields, adding to the rhythm of the day as the sun sets and bonfires are lit.

Beltane is a time for celebrating fertility – not just of the land, but of life itself. The Maypole dance, with its intertwined ribbons, is a well-known fertility symbol, representing the phallic and generative powers of nature. Bonfires, lit to purify and protect, were once thought to ward off evil spirits and encourage the health of crops and livestock. In ancient times, couples would leap over the flames as a symbol of good fortune, fertility and the strengthening of their bond. Handfasting ceremonies, or Pagan weddings, are also commonly held on this day, further symbolizing the union of life and love.

As the heat of summer approaches, Beltane invites us to celebrate vitality, passion and the exuberance of life. It's a time for gatherings in nature, picnics with friends and connecting with the joyous energy of the season. The fires of Beltane inspire renewal, and the energy of the day is a reminder to embrace the fullness of life, creativity and community.

PICKLED PINEAPPLE WEED PIZZA WITH LADY'S SMOCK CASHEW RICOTTA

PLAYING WITH FIRE

Lady's smock, also known as cuckoo flower, can be found growing in damp meadows and woodlands across Europe and North America in the early spring months, often blooming in April and May. Its crown of pale pink flowers may look delicate but the taste is potent and peppery – the perfect symbol of Beltane's connection to fire. Pineapple weed, with its sweet, pineapple-like scent, is a wild herb that flourishes in disturbed areas such as roadsides and fields, often sprouting in early spring. This pizza is more than a meal; it's a way to reconnect with nature's rhythms, cooking over fire while incorporating the energy of wild plants that grow around us during this magical time of year. If you have access to a wood-fired oven to cook this pizza I recommend doing so, Beltane is a fire festival after all.

MAKES 2 MEDIUM PIZZAS (SERVES 4)

FOR THE PICKLES:
120ml (½ cup) apple cider vinegar
1 tbsp sugar
½ tsp sea salt
1 small beetroot, peeled and thinly sliced
1 red onion, thinly sliced
2 tbsp fresh pineapple weed flowers (just the heads)

FOR THE PIZZA DOUGH:
500g (3¾ cups) plain (all-purpose) flour, plus extra for dusting
7g (¼oz) instant yeast
1 tsp sea salt
300ml (1¼ cups) warm water
1 tbsp olive oil

FOR THE RICOTTA:
150g (5½oz) raw cashews (soaked for 4–6 hours)
120ml (½ cup) water
1 tbsp lemon juice
1 tbsp nutritional yeast
1 garlic clove
A handful of lady's smock flowers, clean and finely chopped
Sea salt and black pepper

FOR THE PIZZA TOPPINGS:
3–4 tbsp tomato purée (paste), slightly loosened into a sauce with water, or a drizzle of olive oil
2 pineapple rings, chopped into chunks
Marinated artichoke hearts, sliced
Fresh rocket (arugula) to garnish
Fresh lady's smock flowers to garnish

To make the pickles, combine the apple cider vinegar, sugar and salt in a small saucepan with 60ml (¼ cup) water. Add the peeled and sliced beetroot for colour. Heat until the sugar dissolves, then remove from heat. Put the sliced red onion and pineapple weed flowers in a heatproof jar and pour over the hot liquid, adding the beetroot too. Let cool, seal and refrigerate for at least an hour.

For the pizza dough, mix the flour, yeast and salt in a bowl. Add the warm water and olive oil, stir into a dough, knead for 8–10 minutes until smooth. Cover with a damp cloth and let it rise for an hour or until doubled in size. Once risen, punch down and form back into a ball. Cut into two balls and roll each one out on a floured surface to form two 25-cm (10-inch) wide pizza bases.

While the dough is rising, make the cashew ricotta. Drain the soaked cashews and blend with 120ml (½ cup) water, the lemon juice, nutritional yeast, garlic, lady's smock flowers and salt and pepper until smooth.

Preheat the oven to 220°C/425°F/Gas 7.

Spread the tomato sauce over the pizza bases (or just drizzle the bases with olive oil if preferred), then top with the pickled onion and pineapple weed, chopped pineapple chunks, artichoke and dollops of cashew ricotta. Bake for 12–15 minutes until golden.

Before serving, garnish with fresh lady's smock leaves and rocket to add even more peppery fire flavour! Devour while embracing the energy of the fire your pizza has been made with (even if it was cooked in a conventional oven!).

MOON AND STARS BANANA BREAD

PLANTING THE SEEDS OF INTENTION

Traditionally, Beltane is a time for rituals surrounding growth, creation and new life, symbolizing both physical fertility and the fertility of the earth. However, fertility isn't just about pregnancy and crops – it can also represent the birth of new ideas, fresh motivation or the start of new ventures. It's a time to nurture the seeds of creativity and potential within ourselves, celebrating all forms of growth. Bananas are associated with fertility, prosperity and 'fruitfulness'. The nigella seeds, small but plentiful, echo the potential for growth and abundance in all areas of life. This loaf celebrates fertility in all its forms – whether you're cultivating ideas, relationships or simply seeking new beginnings.

SERVES 6–8

3 large black bananas
90ml (6 tbsp) groundnut oil, plus extra for greasing
100g (½ cup) brown sugar, plus extra for sprinkling
4 tbsp nigella seeds
240g (1¾ cups) plain (all purpose) flour
3 tsp baking powder
2 tsp ground cinnamon
1 tsp ground allspice

Preheat the oven to 200°C/400°F/Gas 6 and grease a 900-g (2-lb) loaf pan.

Cut one of your bananas lengthways down the middle so you have a 'moon' shape. Keep one half of this aside and mash the other half, along with the rest of the bananas, with a fork. Add your oil and sugar and continue to mash until everything is combined.

Set aside eight of the nigella seeds on a plate, then add the rest, along with the remaining dry ingredients to the banana mixture and mix to combine. Pour the batter into the prepared loaf pan. Add your 'moon' banana on top and sprinkle some extra sugar on it. Bake uncovered for 20 minutes, then cover with tinfoil and cook for a further 20 minutes.

As you bake, write down eight intentions you wish to achieve – one for each remaining month of the year. Place these in the bottom of a plant pot before covering with soil. Carefully plant your eight nigella seeds into the soil and gently moisten the soil. Over the coming weeks, care for the seeds by watering them and watching them grow, just as your own new ventures or creative projects will develop.

Once your loaf is done cooking, check a skewer inserted into the centre of the cake comes out clean. Leave to cool in the tin before turning out and serving. Bake this when you want to bring about 'fruitfulness' – it's an ideal bake to use the power of Beltane for generating ideas, or new ventures.

NIGELLA SEEDS, ALSO KNOWN AS BLACK CUMIN, ARE REVERED AS A MEDICINAL MIRACLE IN MUCH OF THE WORLD. AN OLD ARAB PROVERB STATES THAT NIGELLA SEED 'CURES ALL BUT DEATH'. SAID TO ENHANCE SPIRITUAL CONNECTION, WELL-BEING AND INNER PEACE, THESE SEEDS ARE TRADITIONALLY USED FOR FLAVOURING CURRIES AND BREADS – THEIR NUTTY FLAVOUR BALANCES THE SWEETNESS OF THE BREAD AND REPRESENTS THE STARS TO THE BANANA'S MOON.

SUMMER SOLSTICE

AROUND JUNE 21ST

A CELEBRATION OF LIGHT

The Summer Solstice, or 'Litha' in Pagan traditions, is a celebration of the longest day of the year, when the sun reaches its highest point in the sky. Rooted in ancient agricultural and spiritual practices, this festival has been marked by cultures around the world. For many, the solstice represents the zenith of light and life, symbolizing abundance, community and the nurturing warmth of the sun.

In Europe, bonfires were lit to honour the sun's strength and to drive away evil spirits. In ancient Rome, the solstice coincided with the Vestalia festival, honouring Vesta, goddess of the hearth, which underscored the community's reliance on domestic and agricultural prosperity. For Norse peoples, it was a time for gatherings, feasting and offerings to deities such as Baldur, the god of light. In China, the solstice marked the height of 'yin' energy and was linked to celebrations of femininity and earth's nourishment.

Modern-day celebrations often continue these traditions in evolved forms. Festivals such as Midsommer in Scandinavia feature dancing, flower wreaths and maypole rituals. In England, thousands gather at ancient sites like Stonehenge to watch the sunrise align with the stones, a powerful connection to humanity's enduring relationship with celestial cycles.

The solstice also has personal and symbolic significance. It invites reflection on the balance of light and dark within ourselves. It's a time to appreciate the fruits of our efforts and nurture our connections with others.

Seasonal foods are integral to solstice festivities, celebrating the earth's peak productivity. Whether through shared meals, outdoor feasts or quiet meditations on nature's bounty, the Summer Solstice encourages gratitude, joy and a deep appreciation for the light that sustains all life.

FAIRY RING MISO MUSHROOM PIE

A MESSAGE TO THE FAIRIES

Summer Solstice is a time when the fairies are believed to be particularly active. A fairy ring is a naturally occurring circle of mushrooms. Said to be places where fairies dance, these circles are considered magical or even dangerous to enter. This pie creates the magic and creativity of a fairy ring without the danger of getting on the fairies' bad side by breaking it!

SERVES 4–6

500g (1lb 2oz) ready-made shortcrust pastry
Plain (all-purpose) flour, for dusting
2 tbsp olive oil
1 large onion, diced
2 garlic cloves, minced
500g (1lb 2oz) mixed mushrooms (such as chestnut/cremini, oyster or portobello), sliced
½ tbsp miso paste
1 tbsp wholegrain mustard
Splash of white wine (optional)
200ml (⅔ cup) vegetable stock
200ml (⅔ cup) single (light) cream
1 tbsp fresh thyme leaves
Sea salt and black pepper

Preheat the oven to 200°C/400°F/Gas 6 and grease a 25-cm (10-inch) pie dish.

Roll out about two-thirds of the pastry on a flour-dusted surface until it is big enough to easily line the dish with plenty of overhang. Use the pastry to line the dish, pressing it gently into the edges and trim the edges. Use the trimmings (and a little of the remaining pastry, if you need to) to create 8–10 little mushrooms for the decoration and set aside.

In a large pan, heat the olive oil over medium heat and sauté the diced onion for about 5 minutes until softened. Add the minced garlic and sliced mushrooms, cooking until the mushrooms release their moisture and become golden brown (about 8–10 minutes).

Stir the miso paste into your mushrooms along with the mustard and splash of white wine (if using), and cook for another minute. Pour in the vegetable stock and simmer for a few minutes, allowing it to reduce slightly. Stir in the cream and fresh thyme, and season with salt and pepper. Remove from the heat and set aside.

Roll out a circular pastry lid for the pie. Pour the creamy mushroom mixture into the pastry-lined pie dish, and top with the pastry lid. Trim any excess pastry and seal the sides by pressing the pastry with your thumb. Arrange the mushroom shapes on top of the pie in a circular arrangement, creating a mushroom 'fairy ring'. Bake in the preheated oven for 25–30 minutes or until the pastry is golden and crispy. Allow to cool slightly before serving.

Before breaking your fairy ring by slicing the pie, acknowledge the fairies and make a wish to them!

BEAUTIFUL AND INTENTIONAL PLATING IS A RITUAL IN ITSELF THAT ENGAGES THE SENSES, ELEVATING A MEAL INTO SOMETHING SACRED. BY CAREFULLY PRESENTING FOOD, YOU TRANSFORM AN ORDINARY DISH INTO A MINDFUL EXPERIENCE. THE COLOURS, TEXTURES AND ARRANGEMENT CREATE HARMONY, HONOURING THE INGREDIENTS. LIKE LIGHTING A CANDLE, IT TURNS YOUR MEAL INTO A PERSONAL OFFERING AND CELEBRATION OF EVERYDAY BEAUTY.

MEADOWSWEET MANGO STICKY RICE

HONOURING THE BALANCE OF LIGHT AND DARK

Meadowsweet, a plant steeped in folklore, embodies the duality between light and dark. Known for its protective and healing properties, it was cherished in Druidic rituals and bridal blessings alike. Its sweet, almond-like fragrance and midsummer blooms make it a perfect addition to this dish, connecting us to the energy of the sun and the harmony of opposites. This recipe is a self-love ritual, a spell that celebrates the balance of light and dark within us. By breaking open a coconut, we symbolically release the pain or burdens of the year so far, honouring both the shadows and the light that shape us, reminding us that there is darkness, even on the lightest of days.

SERVES 4

270g (9½oz) Thai sticky rice
A generous handful of fresh washed meadowsweet (flowers only), or a handful of dried
1 x 400g (14oz) can of coconut milk
1 tbsp cornflour (cornstarch)
1 tsp sea salt
2 tbsp maple syrup
Sesame seeds, to sprinkle
1 ripe mango, peeled, pitted and sliced

YOU WILL ALSO NEED:
A coconut

MY TRAVELS HAVE DEEPLY SHAPED MY LOVE OF COOKING. IN THAILAND, I WAS TAUGHT HOW TO MAKE MANGO STICKY RICE – A DISH THAT'S SINCE BECOME ONE OF MY FAVOURITES. WHILE MOST OF MY RECIPES ARE ROOTED IN MORE LOCAL INGREDIENTS AND TRADITIONS, EXPLORING OTHER CULTURES HAS FUELLED MY CURIOSITY TO EXPERIMENT WITH NEW FLAVOURS AND COOKING TECHNIQUES. EACH CULINARY DISCOVERY FEELS LIKE A CELEBRATION OF THE WORLD'S DIVERSE FOOD HERITAGE.

Soak your rice overnight in cold water (or for 60 minutes in hot water if you're short on time), then rinse it thoroughly until the water runs clear.

Before beginning, prepare your coconut. Hold it and reflect on the year so far. Envision the coconut as a vessel holding any pain, heaviness or unresolved emotions. When ready, break the coconut open with intention, imagining that as it splits, these burdens are released, making space for light, balance and renewal. Reserve the coconut water if desired.

Rinse the rice one last time and place it in a bamboo rice steamer (alternatively you can use a mesh strainer or colander covered with a pan lid). Gently crush a pinch of the meadowsweet flowers between your fingers, releasing their sweet aroma. Reflect on the magical properties of love, protection and healing, and infuse these intentions into the flowers. Sprinkle the flowers into the steamer basket which will allow their essence to mingle with the rice as it cooks. Place the basket over a pan of simmering water and leave to steam for about 30 minutes until the rice is soft.

While the rice steams, divide the coconut milk into two portions. Combine one half with the cornflour and salt in a saucepan, and heat gently while stirring until it thickens. Pour this mixture into a bowl and set it aside. Add the remaining meadowsweet flowers and maple syrup to the remaining coconut milk, and heat gently for about 10 minutes without boiling. Strain out the flowers and set aside the infused milk.

When the rice is cooked, transfer it to a large bowl and stir in the meadowsweet-infused milk, ensuring the rice is fully coated. Let it rest for 20 minutes to absorb the flavours.

Serve the rice inside your coconut halves – the hollow now filled with love and protection. Drizzle the rice with the salted coconut sauce and garnish with sesame seeds and sliced mango. Use this dish to honour the balance of light and dark, and to celebrate the journey of self-love and transformation.

LUGHNASADH

AUGUST 1ST

A TIME FOR GRATITUDE

Lughnasadh marks the beginning of the harvest season and is one of the four major Celtic fire festivals. Named after the god Lugh, a deity associated with skills, crafts and harvests, this festival was traditionally a time to honour the bounty of the land and the interconnectedness between human effort and nature's cycles. According to legend, Lugh established this festival in memory of his foster mother, Tailtiu, who cleared the land of Ireland for agriculture and died from her labours.

Lughnasadh was marked by communal feasting, competitive games, and offerings of the first fruits to ensure continued abundance. Rituals typically took place on hilltops or open fields, where the community would give thanks for the earth's gifts. Athletic competitions, including races and wrestling, symbolized the physical labour of the harvest and the sacrifices necessary to ensure fertility and renewal.

A common tradition was the crafting and offering of loaves made from the first grains, linking the festival to Lammas ('Loaf Mass'), a Christianized celebration that also emphasizes bread and agricultural gratitude. Although they are sometimes used interchangeably, these festivals are distinct.

Today, Lughnasadh is observed by many modern Pagans and nature-focused practitioners as a time to reflect on personal achievements and communal prosperity. Seasonal foods, such as fresh bread and late summer fruits, are prepared to honour the earth's abundance. Whether through feasting, storytelling or expressing gratitude for life's blessings, Lughnasadh serves as a reminder of the balance between hard work and nature's generosity, fostering a sense of community and thankfulness.

FIG AND FENNEL SODA BREAD

HONOURING THE SACRIFICE

Lughnasadh marks a time to give thanks for the first fruits, bake bread from the new harvest and engage in community celebrations. Remember, the harvest is both emotional and literal – this is a moment for gratitude and reflection upon the sacrifices you have made throughout the year thus far. Fig trees are present in many folklore creation stories across the world – and it seems fitting that they should come into harvest in late summer and early autumn when the death begins. Figs are pollinated by wasps crawling inside the immature fruit and once inside they are unable to get out. The wasp dies and its body is broken down and absorbed by the fig fruit. This comforting recipe reminds us of the sacrifices we make to ensure abundance; like the wasp in the fig, with death comes new life.

SERVES 4–6

1 tbsp apple cider vinegar
240ml (1 cup) milk
240g (1¾ cups) spelt flour
1 tbsp sugar
½ tsp baking powder
1 tsp bicarbonate of soda (baking soda)
½ tsp sea salt
60g (¼ cup) softened butter
60g (2oz) dried figs, chopped
1 tbsp fennel seeds

Preheat the oven to 200°C/400°F/Gas 6 and grease and a line a 20-cm (8-inch) cake pan.

Pour the apple cider vinegar into the milk and let it sit for 5 minutes to curdle.

Combine all dry ingredients in a bowl. Work the butter in with your fingertips as you would for a crumble. Add the milk and apple cider vinegar mixture to your dry ingredients and combine with your hands. Add your figs and half the fennel seeds and mix. Do not knead the dough, only mix it with your hand until all the ingredients are combined into a shaggy dough. As you do so, set an intention for what you're willing to 'sacrifice' in order to foster growth and abundance in your life – whether that's spending less time on social media to be more present or setting boundaries with a person who takes your energy and doesn't return it. Write this sacrifice down on a small piece of baking parchment.

Transfer the dough to the prepared pan and sprinkle the remaining fennel seeds on top. Cut a cross into the loaf to let the fairies out, then bury your parchment sacrifice deep within the dough. Bake for 25 minutes until golden on top.

Slice up the bread, holding back the parchment to be buried later. Take a slice of your bread and 'sacrifice' it to the land – throwing it outside or into a body of water for the earth to take back (this isn't wasteful as your local wildlife will appreciate the treat!) Eat the bread while it's still warm with cold butter and hot soup, taking stock of your year so far and giving thanks for the sacrifices made to create the abundance you enjoy.

WE ALL LOVE TIME-SAVING GADGETS, AND THERE'S NO SHAME IN USING THEM. HOWEVER, WHEN IT COMES TO MINDFUL, INTENTIONAL COOKING, SOMETIMES THE OLD WAYS CAN BE BEST. KNEADING DOUGH BY HAND, FOR EXAMPLE, OFFERS A THERAPEUTIC RHYTHM AND PROMOTES MINDFULNESS. WHILE I SUPPORT KITCHEN SHORTCUTS, SOMETIMES IT'S WORTH TAKING THE TIME, WORKING INTENTIONALLY AND SAVOURING THE FRUITS OF OUR LABOUR. THIS, IN ITSELF, CAN BE AN ACT OF SACRIFICE – USING UP YOUR PERSONAL ENERGY AND STRENGTH TO GROW AND GAIN.

WILD TRIFLE

THE SWEETNESS OF CHILDHOOD GAMES

Though many people are far removed from growing or foraging food, one fruit remains a staple of the harvest season: the humble blackberry. Picking blackberries from hedgerows and cooking them into jams or pies is a cherished tradition, often passed down through generations. In these simple acts, the art of foraging continues to thrive. Blackberries, often found in wild hedgerows or woodland edges, mark the late summer harvest, appearing from late July through September. Paired with elderberries – harvested in late summer and early autumn – these berries celebrate flower turning to fruit and the abundance of the season. If you are harvesting your own blackberries, set a goal for your foraging. Lughnasadh is a time of games and friendly competition. Challenge yourself or others to harvest as many blackberries as possible in a set time. For every handful of blackberries you collect, give something back to the earth. This could be planting a seed, or speaking a word of gratitude for the abundance provided. This practice connects you to the land, honouring the cycles of abundance and gratitude that reflect the spirit of Lughnasadh.

SERVES 4–6

FOR THE PANDAN SPONGE:
190g (1½ cups less 2 tbsp) flour
200g (1 cup) caster (superfine) sugar
1 tsp baking powder
½ tsp bicarbonate of soda (baking soda)
½ tsp sea salt
240ml (1 cup) milk (I like unsweetened almond in this recipe, but any will work)
80ml (1/3 cup) groundnut oil (or melted coconut oil)
2 tsp apple cider vinegar
1 tbsp pandan extract
1 tsp vanilla extract

FOR THE ELDERBERRY JELLY:
140g (5oz) fresh elderberries (make sure to remove any stems)
50g (¼ cup) sugar
2 tsp agar-agar powder

TO ASSEMBLE:
240ml (1 cup) double (heavy) cream of choice
2 tbsp icing (powdered) sugar
100g (3½oz) fresh blackberries

Preheat the oven to 180°C/350°F/Gas 4 and grease and line a 20-cm (8-inch) cake pan.

In a large bowl, mix together the flour, sugar, baking powder, bicarbonate of soda and salt. In another bowl, combine the milk, oil, vinegar, pandan extract and vanilla. Gradually pour the wet mixture into the dry, stirring until just combined. Pour the batter into the prepared pan and bake for 25–30 minutes, until a toothpick inserted into the centre of the cake comes out clean. Remove from the tin after a few minutes of cooling and leave to cool completely on a wire rack before slicing into cubes.

For the elderberry jelly, put the elderberries and sugar in a saucepan with 240ml (1 cup) water and simmer for 10 minutes until they are soft and breaking down. Remove from the heat. Mix the agar-agar with 2 tablespoons cold water, add it to the elderberry liquid and stir until dissolved. Leave to cool slightly in the pan until just warm. Pour into four large wine glasses and let cool in the fridge for 1–2 hours.

When you're ready to assemble, whip the cream with icing sugar until soft peaks form.

On top of the elderberry jelly in your glasses, add the cubed pandan sponge, then the whipped cream and blackberries on top. Refrigerate for at least 30 minutes before serving. Enjoy in the summer sunshine, hold a picnic and play games, savouring the heat and light before it diminishes.

BLACKBERRIES ARE ASSOCIATED WITH CERTAIN FOLKLORIC BELIEFS, ONE BEING THAT THEY SHOULD NOT BE EATEN AFTER SEPTEMBER 29TH, THE FEAST OF ST MICHAEL. AFTER THIS DATE, THE DEVIL'S INFLUENCE MAKES THE FRUIT UNFIT FOR CONSUMPTION: HAVING BEEN CAST OUT OF HEAVEN, HE LANDED ON A BLACKBERRY BUSH AND CURSED THE BERRIES, MAKING THEM BITTER AND HARMFUL. ALTHOUGH THIS IS SUPERSTITION, IT IS TRUE THAT BLACKBERRIES ARE NOT AT THEIR BEST TOWARD THE END OF THE SEASON AS THEY OFTEN SUCCUMB TO FUNGUS!

AUTUMN EQUINOX

AROUND SEPTEMBER 21ST

REAPING THE REWARDS

The Autumn Equinox, often referred to as 'Mabon' in modern Pagan traditions, marks the balance between day and night as the Earth transitions into the darker half of the year. Falling around September 21–23 in the northern hemisphere, it is a time to celebrate harvests, express gratitude for abundance, and prepare for the coming winter. However, it is important to approach the term Mabon with care and respect. While the name is widely used, it originates from a figure in Welsh mythology – Mabon ap Modron, a god associated with youth and light, whose direct connection to the Autumn Equinox is not historically substantiated. Mindfulness around the use of this term helps preserve the diversity and integrity of ancient traditions, avoiding homogenization or misinterpretation.

Harvest festivals have been observed across cultures, reflecting humanity's deep relationship with the land. In Britain, communities gathered to honour the fruits of their labour with offerings to deities of fertility and agriculture. In Greek mythology, the story of Demeter and Persephone symbolizes the seasonal shifts, with Persephone's descent into the Underworld marking the approach of winter. In East Asia, the Mid-Autumn Festival celebrates the full moon and harvest through communal feasts and symbolic foods.

Modern observances of the Autumn Equinox blend ancient practices with contemporary reflection. Celebrations often include feasting, gratitude rituals and reconnecting with nature's cycles. By respecting the roots of these traditions and seeking to understand their cultural contexts, we can honour their original meanings while finding relevance in today's world. This is a time to pause, reflect on our accomplishments, and prepare for the slower, introspective season ahead.

HARVEST SQUASH CORNUCOPIA

A TABLE ALTAR OF ABUNDANCE

The cornucopia, or 'horn of plenty', symbolizes abundance and gratitude, a theme echoed in many harvest festivals throughout history and the world. In modern-day Paganism, the altar is traditionally used as a sacred space to honour deities or intentions – in this recipe it is reimagined as a communal table laden with food and natural treasures. As you prepare this dish, embrace the concept of the cornucopia as a symbol of not just physical abundance, but the prosperity of relationships, ideas and personal growth. This recipe integrates this concept, encouraging you to create a 'table altar' adorned with autumnal offerings such as acorns, leaves and seasonal plants. Ask each guest to bring a contribution to the table, celebrating abundance with a shared harvest of both food and fellowship. Let your table become the sacred altar of your gathering – a visual and culinary feast. Use your squash as the focal point, surrounded by vibrant fruits, nuts and foliage. This feast is both for the eyes and the bellies.

SERVES 4

1 large butternut or harlequin squash
100g (3½oz) pearl barley
400ml (1¾ cups) vegetable broth or water
2 tbsp olive oil
1 small onion, diced
2 garlic cloves, minced
1 x 400g (14oz) can of cannellini beans, drained
60g (2oz) pomegranate seeds
1 tsp dried thyme
60g (2oz) chopped walnuts
80g (2¾oz) dried cranberries or raisins for sweetness (optional)
Fresh herbs, to garnish
Sea salt and black pepper

Preheat your oven to 200°C/400°F/Gas 6. Slice the squash in half lengthwise and scoop out the seeds. Place the halves, cut sides down, on a baking sheet and roast for 30–40 minutes, or until tender.

While the squash roasts, rinse the pearl barley under cold water. In a saucepan, combine the barley and vegetable broth, bringing it to a boil. Reduce the heat and simmer for about 30 minutes, or until the barley is tender and most of the liquid has been absorbed.

In a skillet, heat the olive oil over medium heat and sauté the diced onion and minced garlic until translucent. Once the barley is cooked, add it to the skillet along with the cannellini beans, pomegranate seeds and dried thyme, and season with salt and pepper, stirring to combine. Fold in the chopped nuts and dried cranberries or raisins for added texture and sweetness, if using.

When the squash is done roasting, carefully flip the halves over and fill each one with the barley mixture, pressing down gently to pack it in. Return the filled squash to the oven for an additional 10–15 minutes to heat through.

Once ready, garnish with fresh herbs and serve warm as a beautiful centrepiece for your harvest feast. This combination of communal ritual and mindful preparation transforms your meal into a sacred altar of abundance and connection. Enjoy with friends and take stock by sharing some of the things you have been grateful for in the year so far.

IN GREEK MYTHOLOGY, THE POMEGRANATE SYMBOLIZES LIFE AND DEATH, LINKED TO THE STORY OF PERSEPHONE'S ABDUCTION BY HADES. WHEN SHE EATS SIX SEEDS IN THE UNDERWORLD, SHE IS BOUND TO HADES FOR SIX MONTHS EACH YEAR, REPRESENTING THE CYCLE OF LIFE, DEATH AND REBIRTH. THE FRUIT THUS EMBODIES THE DUALITY OF EXISTENCE – GROWTH AND FERTILITY, AS WELL AS THE INEVITABILITY OF DEATH. THIS CONNECTION TO THE CHANGING SEASONS MAKES THE POMEGRANATE A SYMBOL OF LIFE'S CYCLICAL NATURE.

BAKED MASH WITH SALTED MAPLE, PECAN AND CHILLI CRUST

CHARGING WITH WARMTH AND SIMPLICITY

As the vibrant warmth of summer fades and the crisp autumn air sets in, our meals often shift to reflect the changing season. The importance of adding sweetness and heat into food becomes paramount – these flavours can evoke warm and cozy comfort during the cold months of autumn and winter. Combining sweet potatoes with the crunch of salted maple pecans and a hint of chilli flakes offers a warming, flavourful dish that nourishes both body and spirit. Inspired by the practice of charging objects with intent in folk magic, you can transform the act of preparing this dish into a mindful celebration of autumn's abundance. The simple ritual of charging your ingredients with mindful intention is an easy way to sow some ceremony into each meal.

SERVES 4 (AS A SIDE DISH)

4 medium sweet potatoes
2 tbsp butter
60g (2oz) pecans, crushed
2 tbsp maple syrup, plus optional extra to drizzle
1 tsp chilli flakes, plus optional extra to sprinkle
2 tsp flaked sea salt
Sea salt and black pepper
Fresh herbs, such as parsley or chives, to garnish (optional)

YOU WILL ALSO NEED:
A candle

Before beginning, gather your ingredients and set the intention of warmth and comfort. Light a candle and place it near your cooking space to symbolize the hearth, a timeless source of nourishment and connection. Take a moment to visualize charging these ingredients with your intentions.

Preheat your oven to 200°C/400°F/Gas 6. Pierce the sweet potatoes with a fork and place them on a baking sheet. Bake for 45–60 minutes, or until tender. Once cooked, let them cool slightly before peeling off the skins.

In a mixing bowl, mash the sweet potatoes with the butter and salt and pepper until smooth and creamy. Spread the mash into a baking dish, smoothing the top.

In a separate bowl, combine the crushed pecans, maple syrup, chilli flakes and flaked sea salt, mixing until the pecans are well coated. Sprinkle the pecan mixture evenly over the sweet potato mash. Bake for 15–20 minutes, or until the crust is golden and fragrant.

Garnish with fresh herbs and extra chilli flakes, if you want more heat, and drizzle with extra maple syrup if desired – visualizing the warming, comforting charge they contain. This recipe is the epitome of autumn comfort food, providing a satisfying side that invites everyone to gather around the table.

STICKY APPLE CIDER CARAMEL CAKE

EMBRACING TRANSFORMATION

Apples have long symbolized health, abundance and the cycles of life. In folklore, they embody both nourishment and temptation, from the Garden of Eden to Snow White's poisoned apple. Historically, apples played a key role in harvest celebrations, particularly during the Autumn Equinox, marking growth's transition to dormancy. Apples are also linked to magical practices, believed to protect and attract love. This sticky apple cider caramel cake is more than just a treat; it honours the harvest and invites abundance. As you prepare it, embrace the transformative energy of the season, weaving intention into every step. Before dicing your apples, peel one of them carefully, attempting to create as long an unbroken apple peel as possible. Ask a question and toss this peel onto your work surface to reveal an answer in the shape it creates.

SERVES 6

FOR THE CAKE:
240g (1¾ cups) plain (all-purpose) flour
200g (1 cup) brown sugar
1 tsp baking powder
1 tsp bicarbonate of soda (baking soda)
A pinch of sea salt
100ml (scant ½ cup) unsweetened smooth apple sauce
240ml (1 cup) apple cider (or apple juice if you prefer an alcohol-free version)
60ml (¼ cup) vegetable oil, plus extra for greasing
225g (8oz) diced apples (preferably sweet varieties)

FOR THE APPLE CIDER CARAMEL:
240ml (1 cup) apple cider (or apple juice)
240g (8½oz) coconut cream
200g (1 cup) brown sugar

IN SOME WELSH FOLKLORE, ENCHANTED APPLES WERE SAID TO GRANT ETERNAL YOUTH OR MAGICAL POWERS. THESE APPLES WERE OFTEN FOUND IN FAIRY REALMS OR GUARDED BY MAGICAL CREATURES, REFLECTING THE MYSTICAL IMPORTANCE OF FRUIT IN LOCAL LEGENDS.

Preheat your oven to 180°C /350°F/Gas 4. Grease a 23-cm (9-inch) round cake pan and line the bottom with baking parchment.

In a mixing bowl, combine the dry ingredients for the cake. In another bowl, mix together the apple sauce, apple cider (or juice) and vegetable oil. Gently fold the wet ingredients into the dry ingredients until just combined, being careful not to over mix. Finally, stir in the diced apples, allowing them to distribute evenly throughout the batter.

Pour the batter into the prepared cake pan and bake in the preheated oven for 30–35 minutes, or until a toothpick inserted into the centre of the cake comes out clean.

While the cake is baking, you can prepare the apple cider caramel. In a saucepan, reduce the apple cider (or juice) over medium heat until it thickens and caramelizes, then stir in the coconut cream and brown sugar, and cook until the mixture becomes smooth and creamy.

Once the cake is done, allow it to cool in the pan for a few minutes before transferring it to a wire rack. While the cake cools, take a moment to set your intention for the ritual, perhaps lighting a candle to honour the change of seasons. Once the cake has cooled completely, drizzle the warm apple cider caramel over the top, letting it cascade down the sides.

Serve the cake with love and gratitude, sharing it with friends or family while reflecting on the abundance of the season. As you enjoy each slice, remember to honour the journey of growth and transformation that autumn brings.

SAMHAIN

OCTOBER 31ST

HONOURING THE ANCESTORS

Samhain, celebrated from October 31st to November 1st, is a festival with deep roots in Celtic traditions, particularly in Ireland, Scotland and Wales. The name 'Samhain' translates to 'summer's end', marking the transition from the light of summer to the darkness of winter. It was believed that on this night, the boundary between the physical world and the spirit world was at its thinnest, allowing the souls of the dead to return to visit their families. The Celts honoured their ancestors through rituals, feasting and offerings to the spirits, often lighting bonfires and carving turnips to ward off harmful spirits.

In ancient times, Samhain was a time of harvest and preparation for the cold months ahead, symbolizing the cycle of life, death and rebirth. Traditionally, communities would gather around large bonfires for warmth and protection, and the extinguishing of home hearth fires was followed by a communal relighting of the flame from the sacred bonfire to purify and protect the family for the coming year.

Today, Samhain has evolved into the widely recognized holiday of Halloween, with many of the ancient traditions still alive in modern practices. In Ireland and Scotland, people still celebrate with community gatherings, bonfires and rituals to honour their ancestors. While Halloween in many parts of the world has become commercialized, the spiritual roots of Samhain remain a meaningful time for reflection, remembrance and connection with those who have passed. This festival encourages us to honour our lineage, remember the wisdom of the past, and embrace the cyclical nature of life.

PUMPKIN GNOCCHI BAKE

HONOURING OUR ANCESTORS

The pumpkin, a symbol of harvest and abundance, has deep roots in folklore, especially around Halloween and Samhain. Originating in ancient North America, pumpkins were celebrated for their culinary uses and magical properties. Carved into jack-o'-lanterns, they were believed to ward off evil spirits during the darker months. Beyond festive traditions, pumpkins symbolize nourishment, fertility and the transition into winter. Rich in vitamins and antioxidants, they embody the cyclical nature of life and death. This recipe seeks to blend the process of making a warming autumnal meal with the tradition of carving a pumpkin, whilst paying mindful homage to the ancient root of the festival, by honouring an ancestor.

SERVES 4

FOR THE PUMPKIN GNOCCHI:
50g (1/3 cup) semolina
240g (8½oz) pumpkin purée
180g (1 1/3 cups) 00 pasta flour (plus extra for dusting)
¼ tsp ground nutmeg
½ tsp sea salt
¼ tsp black pepper
1 tbsp olive oil

FOR THE BAKE:
1 tbsp olive oil
1 medium onion, diced
2 garlic cloves, minced
30g (1oz) spinach, chopped
75g (2½oz) cherry tomatoes, halved
1 tsp dried thyme
1 tsp dried sage
50g (3½ tbsp) butter
2 tbsp plain (all-purpose) flour
240ml (1 cup) unsweetened milk
2 tbsp nutritional yeast flakes
50g (1 cup) fresh breadcrumbs
100g (3½oz) cheese of choice, finely grated
Sea salt and black pepper

YOU WILL ALSO NEED:
A pumpkin
A small candle

Begin by carving a pumpkin with a sigil or symbol that represents a lost loved one, or to honour the spirit of your ancestors more generally. As you carve, focus on the symbolism of the pumpkin and connecting to the past. Place a small candle inside the pumpkin and light it, allowing the flame to illuminate your intentions as you cook.

For the gnocchi, start by dusting a tray with the semolina and set aside. Combine the pumpkin purée, flour, nutmeg, salt and black pepper in a bowl, adding the olive oil until a soft dough forms. Knead until smooth, then divide into manageable portions and roll into 2.5-cm (1-inch) thick ropes, then cut each rope into 2.5-cm (1-inch) pieces. Press a fork on each piece to create ridges, then place them on tray with the semolina to stop them sticking.

Preheat the oven to 200°C/400°F/Gas 6. Pre-grease a baking dish.

For the bake, heat the oil in a skillet, and sauté the onion for a few minutes until translucent. Add the garlic, spinach and tomatoes and cook for a further 2–3 minutes until the spinach is wilted. Add the thyme and sage, and season with salt and pepper. Add the butter and let it melt, then add the flour to create a paste. Add the milk a little and a time, continuing to stir so a sauce forms. Fold in the nutritional yeast and gnocchi. Once the gnocci is coated in sauce, transfer the mixture to a greased baking dish, sprinkle with the breadcrumbs and cheese, and bake for 25–30 minutes until golden and crispy on top.

As the dish bakes, set the table with an extra place for a lost loved one or to represent your ancestors. Place the pumpkin on the table as a mindful centrepiece. Let the dish cool slightly before serving – this dish is a comforting celebration of the season, nourishing both body and spirit.

TRADITIONALLY, SAMHAIN IS A TIME FOR STORYTELLING, RITUALS AND CONNECTING WITH THE SPIRIT WORLD.

MEMENTO MORI ROSEMARY SOUL CAKES

REMEMBERING THOSE WHO HAVE PASSED

Soul cakes were originally made to represent a soul in Purgatory – eating a cake was thought to release the soul into Heaven. Traditionally made during the Samhain festival, when the veil is thin, the custom of making soul cakes dates back to the Middle Ages when the cakes were given to 'soulers', who would go door to door, singing prayers for the dead in exchange for food – this is believed to be the origin of trick or treating. The act of sharing these cakes fostered a sense of community while paying homage to those who have left us. Rosemary, often linked with remembrance and fidelity, adds a poignant touch to this ritual. Placing fresh rosemary leaves on the cakes can symbolize the eternal bond between the living and the deceased. This recipe is a way to honour an old tradition and to remember our loved ones who have passed.

MAKES 6 LARGE SOUL CAKES

250g (1¾ cups plus 2 tbsp) plain (all-purpose) flour, plus extra for dusting
100g (½ cup) sugar
1 tsp baking powder
1 tsp ground cinnamon
½ tsp ground nutmeg
¼ tsp sea salt
100ml (scant ½ cup) milk
50ml (3½ tbsp) vegetable oil
2 tbsp chopped fresh rosemary leaves
Finely grated zest of 1 lemon
A handful of dried fruit (such as currants, dried cranberries or raisins)

YOU WILL ALSO NEED:
A candle

Preheat the oven to 180°C/350°F/Gas 6 and line a baking tray with baking parchment.

In a large bowl, stir together the flour, sugar, baking powder, cinnamon, nutmeg and salt. In a separate bowl, combine the milk, vegetable oil, rosemary and lemon zest. Pour the wet ingredients into the dry mixture, stirring until a soft dough forms.

Turn the dough out onto a floured surface and gently knead until smooth. Divide the dough into 6 equal portions and shape them into round cakes, about 2.5cm (1 inch) thick. Place the cakes on the prepared baking tray.

Before placing the cakes in the oven, draw the initial of a loved one atop each cake with a knife. Gently press fruit into the initials. Light a candle nearby and recite the following incantation aloud:

In this light, I remember you;
In this cake, I honour you;
May your spirit find peace and joy.

Bake for 20–25 minutes, or until golden. Once baked, share the cakes by candlelight, in the presence of a photograph or item to represent those you are remembering. Gather with family or friends to reflect on their lives, sharing stories and creating a warm, sacred space for remembrance.

THE PHRASE 'THE VEIL IS THIN' REFERS TO A TIME WHEN THE BOUNDARY BETWEEN THE PHYSICAL WORLD AND THE SPIRITUAL OR UNSEEN REALMS IS BELIEVED TO BE PARTICULARLY POROUS. DURING THIS PERIOD, WHICH OFTEN COINCIDES WITH THE END OF THE HARVEST SEASON AND FESTIVALS LIKE SAMHAIN OR HALLOWEEN, IT'S THOUGHT THAT SPIRITS, ANCESTORS AND OTHERWORLDLY BEINGS CAN MORE EASILY CROSS INTO OUR WORLD. THIS THINNING OF THE VEIL INVITES REFLECTION, COMMUNICATION WITH THE DEAD, AND DEEP SPIRITUAL CONNECTION, WITH PRACTICES RANGING FROM ANCESTOR ALTARS TO DIVINATION, AS THE ENERGY BETWEEN THE LIVING AND THE DECEASED IS HEIGHTENED.

ROSE HIP HARISSA ROASTED CHICKPEAS

THE PIERCED HEART AT THE THRESHOLD

Rose hips, the vibrant fruit of wild roses, have long been associated with protection, love and vitality in folklore. Known for their striking red–orange colour and a range of health benefits, including being rich in vitamin C, various cultures have used rose hips not only medicinally but also as talismans to ward off negative energies. In witchcraft and English folk magic, a pierced heart was a talisman hung at pathways or thresholds to ward off harm. These charms were often created with a heart (sometimes symbolic, sometimes real) pierced by pins or nails, symbolizing both the transfixing and banishment of malicious forces. Inspired by this practice, this recipe integrates these principles using rose hips in place of a heart, harnessing their natural protective qualities.

SERVES 4 (AS A SIDE DISH)

80g (2¾oz) fresh rose hips, plus 7 extra for the ritual
1 red (bell) pepper
2 tbsp olive oil
2 x 400g (14oz) cans of chickpeas, drained and rinsed
2 tsp smoked paprika
1 tsp ground cumin
1 tsp ground coriander (cilantro)
1 tsp garlic powder
½ tsp sea salt
½ tsp black pepper
1 tsp maple syrup (optional)
Juice of 1 lemon (optional)

YOU WILL ALSO NEED:
7 needles
Twine

Before preparing this dish, set aside seven intact rose hips from the harvest. Thread a needle through each one and string them together to hang at your door. In English and broader European folk practices, seven knots were tied into cords to 'trap' negative forces or seal protective intentions. Over the winter, as your seven pierced rose hips dry, they will absorb and ward off negative energy, maintaining a protective barrier for your home.

Preheat the oven to 200°C/400°F/Gas 6.

To make the harissa, halve the fresh rose hips and remove their irritating hairs and seeds. Put the them in a baking tray along with the whole red bell pepper. Drizzle with the olive oil, season with salt and pepper and toss to coat. Roast for 20–30 minutes until everything is soft and charred. Blend the roasted ingredients with the smoked paprika, cumin, coriander, garlic powder, salt and pepper to create a vibrant harissa paste.

Toss the drained chickpeas in the harissa and spread them out on a baking parchment-lined baking tray. Roast for 25–30 minutes, tossing halfway through, until golden and crispy. If desired, drizzle with maple syrup and fresh lemon juice before serving, symbolizing consuming the protective qualities imbued within this dish. The pierced rose hip ritual complements the warmth of the dish, which nourishes and safeguards in equal measure.

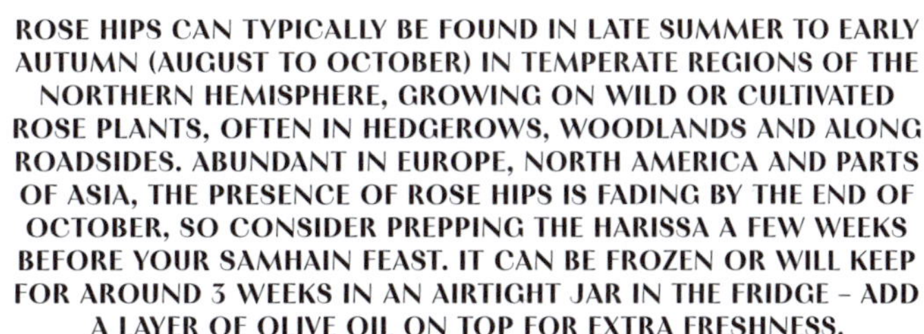

ROSE HIPS CAN TYPICALLY BE FOUND IN LATE SUMMER TO EARLY AUTUMN (AUGUST TO OCTOBER) IN TEMPERATE REGIONS OF THE NORTHERN HEMISPHERE, GROWING ON WILD OR CULTIVATED ROSE PLANTS, OFTEN IN HEDGEROWS, WOODLANDS AND ALONG ROADSIDES. ABUNDANT IN EUROPE, NORTH AMERICA AND PARTS OF ASIA, THE PRESENCE OF ROSE HIPS IS FADING BY THE END OF OCTOBER, SO CONSIDER PREPPING THE HARISSA A FEW WEEKS BEFORE YOUR SAMHAIN FEAST. IT CAN BE FROZEN OR WILL KEEP FOR AROUND 3 WEEKS IN AN AIRTIGHT JAR IN THE FRIDGE – ADD A LAYER OF OLIVE OIL ON TOP FOR EXTRA FRESHNESS.

BLACK MAGIC CAKE

TRANSFORMING NEGATIVITY

Throughout history, the term 'Black Magic' has been fraught with misconceptions and fear, often unfairly labelling practitioners of witchcraft as inherently malevolent. In a time when we no longer fear black magic as a reality, it is essential to remember that the energies we encounter can still hold both positive and negative influences. Therefore, incorporating protective rituals into our practices remains relevant, allowing us to stand strong against any unwelcome intentions. This Black Magic Cake is a celebration of how modern witches are reclaiming the knowledge of our ancestors – once persecuted – and turning it into something positive.

SERVES 6–8

250g (1¾ cups plus 2 tbsp) plain (all-purpose) flour
200g (1 cup) caster (superfine) sugar
100g (1 cup) cocoa powder
1 tsp bicarbonate of soda (baking soda)
½ tsp sea salt
300ml (1¼ cups) milk
100ml (scant ½ cup) vegetable oil
1 tsp vanilla extract
Black food colouring (optional)
Redcurrants and blackthorn leaves

FOR THE BLACKTHORN BERRY JAM:
200g (7oz) fresh blackthorn (sloe) berries, cleaned, de-stoned and chopped (you can use plums as an alternative)
100g (½ cup) caster (superfine) sugar

FOR THE SWEET CHESTNUT BUTTERCREAM:
200g (¾ cup plus 2 tbsp) butter, softened
250g (1¾ cups) icing (powdered) sugar
100g (3½oz) sweet chestnut purée
1–2 tbsp milk (optional)
Black food colouring (optional)

YOU WILL ALSO NEED:
A white candle

BLACKTHORN IS OFTEN LINKED TO PROTECTIVE MAGIC AND THE COUNTERACTION OF DARK FORCES. ITS THORNS SYMBOLIZED THE BOUNDARY BETWEEN THIS WORLD AND THE OTHER, SERVING AS A NATURAL DEFENCE AGAINST ILL-INTENT AND MALEVOLENT SPIRITS.

As you prepare the Black Magic Cake, infuse it with your own intention for protection. Begin by lighting a white candle as a symbol of purity and safety. As you mix your ingredients, recite the following incantation:

With this flame, I shield my space,
Only love shall enter this place
In this cake, strength shall be found,
As I walk this sacred ground.

Preheat your oven to 180°C/350°F/Gas 4 and grease two 20-cm (8-inch) round cake pans. Sift the flour, sugar, cocoa powder, bicarbonate of soda and salt into a large bowl.

In a separate bowl, whisk together the milk, vegetable oil and vanilla extract. Combine the wet and dry ingredients, stirring until smooth. Add black food colouring, if desired, stirring until you have an even colour.

Pour the batter into the prepared pans and bake for 30–35 minutes, or until a toothpick inserted into the centre of the cakes comes out clean. Remove the cakes from their pans and let them cool on a wire rack.

For the blackthorn berry jam, put the blackthorn berries and sugar in a saucepan with 100ml (scant ½ cup) water and simmer for 20 minutes, mashing the berries as they cook to break them down. Once the mixture is thickened, remove from the heat and set aside to cool in the pan.

For the chestnut buttercream, whip together the butter and icing sugar, then mix in the chestnut purée, adjusting with a splash of milk if needed to loosen. Add black food colouring if desired.

To assemble the cake, spread blackthorn jam on one cake, then top with a layer of buttercream, and place the second cake on top. Frost the top and sides of the cake with the remaining buttercream and decorate with redcurrants and blackthorn leaves.

WINTER SOLSTICE

AROUND DECEMBER 21ST

REFLECTION AND RENEWAL

The Winter Solstice, marking the longest night and the return of light, is a moment of reflection and renewal. It has deep roots in ancient traditions, with cultures around the world observing this time as a symbol of rebirth and hope. For centuries, the solstice has been celebrated as a time when the dark half of the year reaches its peak, and from that point onward, the days gradually lengthen, heralding the return of the sun.

In pre-Christian Europe, the Winter Solstice was celebrated as Yule, a festival honouring the rebirth of the sun. The Norse celebrated with feasts and the burning of the Yule log, a tradition symbolizing warmth, protection and the promise of brighter days ahead. The Celts also recognized the solstice as a moment of renewal. In many traditions, the solstice was a time for quiet reflection, looking inward and setting intentions for the new year.

In modern times, the Winter Solstice remains a time for connecting with loved ones and embracing stillness. It's an opportunity to pause, reflect on the year gone by, and rest before the active energy of the new year takes hold. Celebrations often include lighting candles, sharing comforting food, and engaging in rituals that honour the return of the light. The solstice reminds us that even in the darkest times, the promise of new beginnings is always on the horizon, and by observing this natural cycle, we can align ourselves more closely with the rhythms of the earth.

Through these rituals, we cultivate a deeper appreciation for the cycles of life, finding hope and strength in the seasons of renewal.

CREAM CHEESE, CARAMELIZED LEEK AND NUTMEG GALETTE

A FOCUS ON YOUR INTENTIONS

The rich cream cheese in this galette offers comfort during the coldest months, while the caramelized leek symbolizes the death and rebirth of winter. Nutmeg, a spice tied to solstice traditions, adds a warming, festive touch. As the solstice marks the quiet beauty of the longest night, this galette honours the season's spirit – nourishing and full of warmth, perfect for cozy gatherings as we await the return of brighter days. The folds of this galette are a mindfulness exercise in bringing intentional awareness to the your intentions set on Imbolc at the beginning of the year; now is the time to retrieve your written intentions and assess them.

SERVES 4–6

500g (1lb 2oz) block of puff pastry
2 tbsp butter
2 leeks, thinly sliced
½ tsp ground nutmeg
200g (7oz) cream cheese of choice
1 tsp chilli flakes
A few sprigs of fresh thyme, plus optional extra to garnish
Sea salt and black pepper
Fresh rosemary, to garnish (optional)

Begin by preheating your oven to 200°C/400°F/Gas 6.

Roll out the pastry on a sheet of baking parchment, shaping it into a 23-cm (9-inch) circle, then slide the parchment onto a large baking tray.

In a skillet, melt the butter over medium heat, add the sliced leeks, and cook until soft and caramelized. Season with the nutmeg and salt and pepper.

Spread cream cheese evenly over the pastry circle, leaving a 2.5-cm (1-inch) border around the edge. Roll the leek slices and place on top, then fold the edges of the pastry over the filling to create a rustic galette.

As you fold, take a moment to reflect on the intentions you've set for the year. With each fold, tuck a single leaf of thyme under the pastry as a symbol of healing and renewal – reading aloud your intentions set on Imbolc one by one. Express gratitude for those that have come to fruition, and contemplation for those that have not.

Sprinkle with chilli flakes and bake for 25–30 minutes until golden brown. As the galette bakes, the folded pastry edges will rise, symbolizing the release of gratitude or letting go of what no longer serves you.

Once out of the oven, allow it to cool slightly. Garnish with fresh thyme or rosemary, then serve with loved ones, embracing the symbolism of growth and release, and the nourishment of both body and spirit.

LEEKS SYMBOLIZE VITALITY, PROTECTION AND REBIRTH IN FOLKLORE. THEIR NOURISHING PROPERTIES HELP STRENGTHEN THE IMMUNE SYSTEM DURING THE COLD MONTHS, AND THEIR WARMING QUALITIES ARE OFTEN LINKED TO HEALING AND VITALITY. THEY ALSO SYMBOLIZE THE RETURN OF LIGHT, WHICH MAKES THEM PERFECT FOR COZY, SOUL-WARMING MEALS AS THEY REPRESENT RENEWAL AND LIFE FORCE IN DARK, COLD TIMES.

CLEMENTINE-SOAKED CARROTS

FOR CLARITY AND REFLECTION

Carrots have long been associated with clear vision, both physically and symbolically. They are believed to enhance not only our sight but also our inner clarity, making them the perfect ingredient for reflection. Winter is a natural time for introspection, a season to slow down and quietly reflect on the year that has passed, seeking clarity about what lies ahead. Root vegetables of all kinds keep us grounded and connected to ourselves and the world around us. This is the perfect recipe ritual to add some vibrant sweetness and mental retrospection into dark gloomy days.

SERVES 4 (AS A SIDE DISH)

300g (10½oz) mixed carrots, peeled and cut into sticks or baby carrots
Juice and finely grated zest of 2 clementines
2 tbsp olive oil
1 tbsp maple syrup
Sea salt and black pepper

YOU WILL ALSO NEED:
A candle, ideally purple
A blindfold
Incense (optional)
A crystal (optional)

Begin by lighting a candle, a symbol of illumination as you reflect on the past year. I like to choose a purple candle for this to engage my deeper thoughts and intuition.

Place the carrot sticks in a roasting pan or dish. In a bowl, whisk together the fresh clementine juice and zest, olive oil and maple syrup, and season with salt and pepper. Pour the clementine mixture over the carrots, ensuring each stick is well-coated. Cover and place in the fridge to marinate for at least 1 hour.

As the carrots marinate, put on a blindfold and sit somewhere quietly to reflect on the year that has passed. You may wish to light some incense and hold a crystal to help you meditate and reflect. Consider what you've learned and what has become clearer to you as the year has unfolded.

Preheat the oven to 200°C/400°F/Gas 6.

After the hour has passed, transfer the carrot pan to the preheated oven and roast for around 40 minutes or until the carrots are soft and caramelizing. Share as part of a Winter Solstice feast and reflect together on what the year has brought to you.

OREGANO OIL ROASTED POTATOES

FOR LETTING GO

As the year draws to a close, it's natural to reflect on what didn't go as planned, and what you may want to release before stepping into the new year. Letting go of past burdens, mistakes or unmet expectations can create space for new beginnings and fresh perspectives. Oregano, a powerful herb long associated with protection and purification, becomes a perfect companion for this time of transition. This recipe invites you to mindfully release what no longer serves you as you savour the comforting warmth of a simple, nourishing dish. The process of preparing the oregano itself becomes a ritual of release, allowing you to symbolically let go with every leaf.

SERVES 4–6 (AS A SIDE DISH)

A small handful of fresh oregano
1kg (2lb 4oz) baby potatoes, halved
3 tbsp olive oil
3 garlic cloves, minced
Sea salt and black pepper

YOU WILL ALSO NEED:
Twine

Preheat your oven to 200°C/400°F/Gas 6.

Mindfully pick each oregano leaf off the stalk, one by one, allowing the leaves to fall into a small bowl as you release your burdens. Set the empty stalks aside, imagining them as the remnants of what you're leaving behind.

Pour the olive oil into a roasting pan and place in the oven. Let the pan sit in the oven for 10 minutes before adding the potatoes to heat up.

Meanwhile, par-boil your potatoes for 7–8 minutes until starting to soften, taking a few deep breaths as they cook to reflect on what you'd like to let go of before the year ends.

Drain your potatoes. Remove the roasting pan from the oven and toss your potatoes into the hot oil, adding your minced garlic and oregano leaves and seasoning with salt and pepper. Roast for 35–40 minutes until golden and crispy.

As the potatoes roast, bind the oregano stalks with twine and hang them to dry, ready to burn on New Year's Day to symbolize new beginnings. When the potatoes are ready, serve them as a grounding and heartwarming dish, welcoming the fresh year ahead with a clear mind and open heart.

YULE LOG WITH PERSIMMON JAM

WELCOMING BACK THE LIGHT

This time of year is not only for reflection and letting go, but also for feasting and celebration! Sharing food and conversation around the dinner table helps us to connect to others in our life. The tradition of the Yule log, burned to bring warmth and good fortune, symbolizes the returning light. This symbol of light during the darkest days of the year is the perfect antidote for anyone, like me, who suffers from low energy and a lack of motivation in the winter months and is a way to invite energy and light into your life!

SERVES 6–8

FOR THE CAKE:
120g (4¼oz) aquafaba
⅛ tsp cream of tartar
125g (2/3 cup less 2 tsp) caster (superfine) sugar, plus 2 tbsp for dusting
180g (1 1/3 cups) plain (all-purpose) flour
1 tbsp ground ginger
1 tsp ground cardamon
1¼ tsp baking powder
A pinch of sea salt
80g (2¾oz) smooth apple sauce
3 tbsp olive oil
2 tbsp milk
1 tsp vanilla extract
Icing (powdered) sugar, for dusting

FOR THE PERSIMMON JAM:
4 ripe persimmons (approx. 500g/1lb 2oz), peeled and chopped
150g (¾ cup) caster (superfine) sugar
2 tbsp lemon juice
½ tsp ground cinnamon
½ tsp ground ginger

FOR THE BUTTERCREAM:
100g (scant ½ cup) butter, softened
180g (1¼ cups) icing (powdered) sugar
25g (1oz) white chocolate, melted
1 tsp vanilla extract

FOR THE GANACHE:
250g (9oz) white chocolate finely chopped
200ml (generous ¾ cup) double (heavy) cream

TO DECORATE:
Rosemary sprigs
Redcurrants

Start with the persimmon jam. Place the chopped persimmons in a medium saucepan and add the sugar and lemon juice. Cook over medium heat, stirring occasionally, until the sugar dissolves and the fruit begins to break down – about 10–15 minutes. Use a fork or masher to break up the persimmons further. Add the cinnamon and ginger and continue to cook the mixture for another 20–30 minutes, stirring occasionally, until it thickens and reaches a jam-like consistency. Remove from heat and let cool.

Preheat the oven to 200°C/400°F/Gas 6 and line a 23 x 33-cm (9 x 13-inch) baking tin with baking parchment, leaving some overhang.

In a large, clean bowl, beat together the aquafaba and cream of tartar with a whisk until frothy. Gradually add the sugar, whisking until the mixture reaches the consistency of softly whipped cream. Sift the flour, ginger, cardamon, baking powder and salt over the mixture and gently fold in. Add the apple sauce, oil, milk and vanilla, folding in until just combined without knocking too much air out of the mixture. Pour the batter into the prepared tin, level the top, and bake for 8–11 minutes until golden.

While the sponge is baking, dust a large sheet of baking parchment with icing sugar. Once the cake is done, flip it out of the pan onto the prepared parchment and let it cool for about an hour.

For the buttercream, whisk together the butter, icing sugar, melted white chocolate and vanilla until light and fluffy.

Once the cake has cooled, trim the edges and spread the buttercream over the sponge, followed by a layer of the persimmon jam. Roll up the cake from a shorter edge into a log. Chill for at least 2 hours.

For the ganache, melt the chocolate and cream in a heatproof bowl set over a pan of simmering water, then leave to cool until spreadable. Spread the ganache over the cake and decorate with redcurrants and rosemary sprigs.

Serve with friends by abundant candlelight, celebrating the coming return of the sun!

MENSTRUAL MAGIC

RECIPES FOR MENSTRUAL HEALTH

For centuries, women have been closely tied to the moon and the natural world, particularly through their menstrual cycles. These cycles, which mirror the 28-day lunar cycle, have long been considered sacred in many cultures, symbolizing renewal, intuition and even spiritual power. In ancient times, menstruation was seen as a potent time for introspection and magic.

Historically, reproductive health was primarily managed by women – healers, midwives and herbalists who had intimate knowledge of women's bodies. However, during the witch hunts, many of these women became targets of persecution. Scholars have argued that this was, in part, a way to strip women of their autonomy and knowledge about their own health, shifting control to patriarchal institutions.

Superstitions around menstruation have also shaped societal attitudes toward women's health. In medieval Europe, menstruating women were often seen as dangerous or unclean, and many were isolated due to fears of bad luck or harm. While these superstitions were largely rooted in ignorance, they reinforced pernicious beliefs that women's bodies were unpredictable or to be feared. Contemporary witches and feminists today are revisiting these narratives, reclaiming menstruation and somatic cycles as sources of power, rather than shame or weakness.

In contemporary magical tales, such as *Frozen* and *Wicked*, emotions are the source of a power – raw, untamed energy that often causes chaos until it is mastered. Similarly, during PMS (premenstrual syndrome), heightened emotions can feel overwhelming, but they hold immense transformative potential.

HARNESSING THE POWER OF OUR CYCLE

By understanding the phases of our cycles, we can harness the particular strengths that align with our magical intentions. What if irritability and mood swings during the menstural phase, for example, were actually a time of heightened intuition?

Similarly, the follicular phase (after menstruation but before ovulation) is often associated with increased energy and radiance, making it a great time to schedule important events, meetings or even social outings that require a boost of self-esteem.

On the flip side, the luteal phase (the days leading up to menstruation) is often marked by fatigue and sluggishness. Rather than fighting against it, we can use this time to rest and reflect.

Of course, not all menstrual symptoms are pleasant. Many women experience extreme pain, fatigue or mental health challenges – particularly those with conditions such as PMDD (premenstrual dysphoric disorder), PCOS (polycystic ovary syndrome) or endometriosis. For these women, menstruation can be a time of immense suffering. Additionally, the transition into menopause, and the perimenopausal period before it, are fraught with hormonal shifts that can cause everything from hot flashes to mood swings, mental health issues and physical discomfort.

Whilst not a substitute for medical treatment, there is a growing movement toward using herbal remedies, mindfulness and ritual to help ease and manage symptoms. Many women have found comfort in rituals that centre their menstrual cycles, using plants such as chamomile for calming properties, or raspberry leaf to ease cramps. These practices empower women to reconnect with their bodies in a holistic, supportive way.

Unfortunately, throughout history, medicine has often neglected women's 'complex' bodies and needs. Studies show that even today, women's pain is frequently dismissed by medical professionals, and conditions such as endometriosis are often misdiagnosed or left untreated for years. Women's health has historically been understudied, leaving gaps in medical knowledge about everything from menstruation to menopause. This lack of understanding has perpetuated the myth that women's bodies are chaotic or unruly.

However, by tuning into our bodies' natural rhythms and working with them rather than against them, we can reclaim our cycles as sources of power and intuition. Modern witches, herbalists and feminists are finding new ways to support menstrual health, both through traditional practices and by advocating for better healthcare.

By embracing our biological rhythms rather than viewing them as obstacles, we can reclaim a vital aspect of ourselves, honouring the ebb and flow of our cycles is a powerful act of self-love and empowerment.

HARNESSING THE WISDOM IN THIS CHAPTER IS NOT EXCLUSIVELY FOR WOMEN OR THOSE WHO MENSTRUATE. THE TEACHINGS WITHIN THESE CHAPTERS CAN ALSO BE APPLICABLE FOR THOSE WHO DO NOT MENSTRUATE OR DO NOT IDENTIFY AS WOMEN. MANY PEOPLE EXPERIENCE THE SYMPTOMS OF MENSTRUATION EVEN IF IT'S NOT DIRECTLY LINKED TO A MENSTRUAL CYCLE – WHATEVER YOUR GENDER IDENTITY OR REPRODUCTIVE STATUS YOU CAN STILL USE THESE RECIPES TO EASE ANXIETY, ENHANCE BEAUTY AND MAGNIFY YOUR INTUITION!

MENSTRUAL PHASE (DAYS 1–5)

PHYSICAL EFFECTS: MENSTRUAL BLEEDING OCCURS, YOU MIGHT EXPERIENCE CRAMPING, BLOATING, FATIGUE AND BACK PAIN.

MENTAL EFFECTS: YOU MAY FEEL LOWER ENERGY LEVELS, MOOD SWINGS OR IRRITABILITY.

FOLLICULAR PHASE (DAYS 6–14)

PHYSICAL EFFECTS: ENERGY LEVELS GENERALLY START TO INCREASE AS THE BODY PREPARES FOR OVULATION. YOU MAY NOTICE IMPROVED SKIN AND DIGESTION.

MENTAL EFFECTS: ENHANCED MOOD AND INCREASED MOTIVATION. COGNITIVE FUNCTION OFTEN IMPROVES DURING THIS PHASE.

OVULATORY PHASE (DAYS 14–16)

PHYSICAL EFFECTS: YOU MAY FEEL ENERGETIC AND HAVE A HIGHER LIBIDO. YOUR SKIN MIGHT LOOK CLEARER DUE TO HORMONAL CHANGES. YOU MAY EXPERIENCE MILD CRAMPING AND CERVICAL MUCAS CHANGES.

MENTAL EFFECTS: OPTIMISM AND CONFIDENCE CAN BE HIGHER DURING THIS TIME.

LUTEAL PHASE (DAYS 17–28)

PHYSICAL EFFECTS: YOU MAY EXPERIENCE PREMENSTRUAL SYMPTOMS SUCH AS BLOATING, MOOD SWINGS AND BREAST TENDERNESS.

MENTAL EFFECTS: MOOD SWINGS, ANXIETY OR IRRITABILITY ARE COMMON DUE TO FLUCTUATING HORMONE LEVELS.

MUGWORT AND BLACK GARLIC FOCACCIA

A DREAM SPELL FOR THE MENSTRUAL PHASE

Mugwort is a staple witch's herb, a perennial of the genus *Artemisia* that has deep roots in folklore and healing. Particularly notable is its historical association with the female reproductive system. Named after the Greek goddess Artemis, who represents the moon and femininity, mugwort has long been revered for its mystical and medicinal properties. Traditionally, it was used to regulate menstrual cycles, ease menstrual cramps and stimulate labour, aligning it with Artemis as a protector of women. Brewed as a tea or infused into oils, mugwort is believed to bring comfort and balance during this time. In addition, it has a long-standing connection to enhancing dreams, which can be useful for women seeking insight. This recipe is not only designed to ease the symptoms of menstruation but the ritual alongside it seeks to enhance the intuitive power of the herb, harnessing the positives of menstruation on the psyche.

SERVES 6–8

500g (3¾ cups) strong white bread flour, plus extra for dusting
7g (¼oz) dried active yeast
1 tbsp sea salt
Around 5 tbsp olive oil
4 tbsp very finely chopped fresh mugwort leaves, plus optional extra sprigs for the top
350ml (1½ cups) lukewarm water
9 black garlic cloves
A sprinkle of sea salt flakes

YOU WILL ALSO NEED:
A small bunch of mugwort, bound with twine
A notebook and pen

DO NOT USE MUGWORT IF YOU ARE PREGNANT OR SEEKING TO BECOME PREGNANT. MUGWORT WAS ALSO USED AS AN ABORTIFACIENT AND CAN STIMULATE LABOUR AND MENSTRUATION.

Add the flour and yeast to a mixing bowl. Mix together, then add your salt and mix in. Make a well in the middle of the flour, add 2 tablespoons of the olive oil and your mugwort and mix while gradually adding your water until you have a sticky dough. If the dough reaches a good consistency before you use all the water, do not add any more.

Flour a surface and tip the dough out. Knead for around 5–10 minutes until it's soft and sticky. Put it back into the bowl, drizzle some oil on top and leave in a warm place, covered by a tea (dish) towel, for an hour.

Grease a 900-g (2-lb) loaf pan with oil. Tip the dough in and stretch it out with your fingers to reach the edges of the pan. Cover again and leave for a further 45 minutes. Toward the end of the proving time, preheat your oven to 200°C/400°F/Gas 6.

Once proved, dimple the bread with your fingers and add the black garlic cloves into some of the holes. Drizzle another 1 tablespoon of oil on top and sprinkle with flaked salt. You might want to add sprigs of fresh mugwort here too. Bake for 20 minutes until golden and crispy. Drizzle with more oil when hot out the oven.

This should ideally be eaten a few hours before bed. Hang mugwort above your bed and place a notebook under your pillow. You may have questions you are seeking intuition and understanding on. Write these in the notebook and go to sleep. Upon waking, write down your dreams – the analysis of these visions could provide you with the answers you seek.

OLIVE OIL CHOCOLATE ORANGE MOUSSE

A GLAMOUR SPELL FOR THE FOLLICULAR PHASE

This phase of the menstrual cycle is marked by rising oestrogen levels. During this time, many women experience enhanced mental clarity, confidence and even beauty – making it an ideal moment for self-care rituals and beauty-enhancing spells. Incorporating foods rich in antioxidants and healthy fats, like olive oil, can support this glow from within. Olive oil has long been celebrated for its association with beauty and health. In ancient Greece, olive trees symbolized endurance, and spilling this revered oil was considered bad luck. Rosemary, too, has a rich history, and is recognized as a herb of remembrance that enhances memory and concentration. Scholars in ancient Greece wore rosemary to boost their focus, while brides embraced its symbolism of fidelity and feminine power. Combining these ingredients in this mousse allows you to challenge the toxic narratives surrounding olive oil as merely high in calories – when it is in fact a potent beauty food.

SERVES 4

50g (1¾oz) dark (bittersweet) chocolate, melted
3 tbsp high-quality rosemary-infused olive oil (see method)
1 tbsp orange zest
1 tsp vanilla extract
25g (¼ cup) cocoa powder
1 tbsp maple syrup (or to taste)
200ml (generous ¾ cup) double (heavy) cream
Small sprigs of rosemary and dried orange slices, to garnish

To make rosemary-infused olive oil, put 240ml (1 cup) olive oil and 3 large fresh rosemary sprigs in a saucepan and set over low heat. Warm the oil gently, keeping the temperature between 50–65°C/120–150°F, for about 5–10 minutes, ensuring it doesn't boil. This allows the rosemary to release its flavour without burning. Once the oil is fragrant, remove it from the heat, let it cool, and strain out the rosemary. Store the infused oil in a sterilized bottle in a cool, dark place for up to 1 month.

To make the mousse, melt the dark chocolate in a heatproof bowl set over a simmering pan of water and whisk in the olive oil until smooth and glossy. Remove from the heat and add the orange zest, vanilla, cocoa powder and maple syrup. Set aside to cool.

In a separate bowl, whip the cream until light and fluffy, then fold it into the cooled chocolate mixture. Spoon the mousse into four glasses and chill for at least 2 hours. When you're ready, garnish with rosemary and orange slices.

For added ritual, place fresh rosemary sprigs in your hair and enjoy this mousse in front of a mirror, repeating an incantation for beauty and self-love:

Glamour flows through me,
both fierce and divine,
In this moment of quiet,
my spirit will shine.
As I honour my body,
my confidence grows,
I am beautiful,
my true self now shows.

You can anoint yourself with the rosemary-infused oil whenever you feel that you need a glamour boost.

THE TERM 'GLAMOUR' ORIGINATES FROM THE SCOTS WORD 'GLAMER', WHICH INITIALLY REFERRED TO A SENSE OF MAGICAL ENCHANTMENT, TIED TO THE IDEA OF ILLUSION. BY THE EARLY 18TH CENTURY, IT EVOLVED TO DESCRIBE AN ALLURING BUT POTENTIALLY DECEPTIVE ATTRACTIVENESS. IN THE EARLY 1900S, ITS MEANING SHIFTED FURTHER TO SIGNIFY A SOPHISTICATED, CAPTIVATING IMAGE, PARTICULARLY ASSOCIATED WITH FEMININITY AND LUXURY, REFLECTING CHANGING SOCIETAL VIEWS ON BEAUTY.

BLACK SCRYING TEA

A SCRYING SPELL FOR THE OVULATORY PHASE

During the ovulatory phase of the menstrual cycle, many experience a surge of confidence, energy and mental clarity. This is an ideal time for divination. This heightened state of awareness makes it easier to tap into your intuition and seek answers to deep questions. With the addition of sage, a herb traditionally linked to wisdom and heightened psychic abilities, this tea encourages you to surrender to your mind's wisdom. In this phase, consider asking questions that truly resonate with your heart, inviting insights that can guide you on your journey. Scrying not only engages your intuition but also celebrates the wisdom of your body and the cyclical rhythms that influence your mind. Each sip deepens your connection to yourself, transforming your question into a journey of self-discovery. Enjoy the soothing flavours and embrace the clarity that comes from within.

SERVES 1

1 teacup of raspberry leaf tea (preferably made with moon water, see page 30)
1 tsp food-grade activated charcoal
1 tsp maple syrup
3 fresh sage leaves
Liquorice root, to stir

YOU WILL ALSO NEED:
A purple candle
A piece of paper and pen
A dark cloth

Begin your ritual by lighting a purple candle. Take a moment to ground yourself before writing down a question on a piece of paper. Brew your tea with the maple syrup and sage leaves, and then pour it into your favourite mug or teacup. Using the liquorice root, stir in the activated charcoal to ward off negativity, clearing your mind of any anxiety that may cloud your intuition.

Next, place the paper with your question under a mirror or your teacup's saucer. Stir your tea seven times anticlockwise, and then seven times clockwise – this will remove any traces of negativity and invite intuition in. Pour a small amount of your prepared tea onto the saucer or mirror, creating a reflective surface. Drape a dark cloth over your head to enhance focus, and gaze at the liquid. Concentrate intently on your question, allowing shapes to form in the liquid to reveal messages and visions.

After a few minutes, your tea will cool enough for you to sip while reflecting on any insights. Pay attention to the pattern of the charcoal grains left in the cup too, as they may provide further guidance. Once you feel satisfied with your exploration, if your question has been answered, burn the paper as a release and blow out the candle. If not, place the paper under your pillow to invite the answers into your dreams.

SCRYING IS A DIVINATION PRACTICE THAT INVOLVES GAZING INTO A REFLECTIVE SURFACE – SUCH AS WATER, MIRRORS OR CRYSTAL – TO SEEK INSIGHTS, VISIONS OR ANSWERS TO QUESTIONS. OFTEN ASSOCIATED WITH MYSTICAL AND SPIRITUAL TRADITIONS, IT TAPS INTO THE INTUITION AND SUBCONSCIOUS MIND. PRACTITIONERS BELIEVE THAT THROUGH THIS PROCESS, THEY CAN ACCESS DEEPER TRUTHS AND CONNECT WITH SPIRITUAL GUIDES. SCRYING CAN ALSO ENHANCE MEDITATION, PROVIDING CLARITY AND FOCUS ON PERSONAL ISSUES. THIS ANCIENT ART HAS ROOTS IN VARIOUS CULTURES, MAKING IT A CHERISHED TOOL FOR SELF-EXPLORATION AND PROPHECY.

MENSTRUAL CALMING CHAMOMILE MILK CAKE

A SOOTHING SPELL FOR THE LUTEAL PHASE

Chamomile has strong ties to menstrual health, known for soothing cramps and balancing hormonal mood swings. The Romans used chamomile specifically for menstrual pain, making it a key player in menstrual magic. Chamomile's calming properties also aid in stress relief, helping the body relax. Its connection to the feminine cycle is ancient, symbolizing fertility, vitality and balance.

SERVES 6–8

300g (2 ¼ cups) plain (all-purpose) flour
75g (6 tbsp) sugar
2 tsp baking powder
½ tsp bicarbonate of soda (baking soda)
½ tsp sea salt
240ml (1 cup) milk of choice
60ml (¼ cup) neutral oil, plus extra for greasing
2 tsp apple cider vinegar
Finely grated zest of 1 lemon
1 tbsp lemon juice
1 tsp vanilla extract

FOR THE MILK SYRUP:
240ml (1 cup) milk of your choice
50g (¼ cup) sugar
3 tbsp dried chamomile
1 tsp ground cinnamon
½ tsp ground turmeric
½ tsp ground ginger
Grated zest of 1 lemon
A tiny pinch of salt

FOR TOPPING:
200ml (generous ¾ cup) double (heavy) cream
2 tbsp icing (powdered) sugar
200g (7oz) strawberries, chopped

YOU WILL ALSO NEED:
A sage green or purple candle

Preheat your oven to 180°C/350°F/Gas 4 and grease a 23cm (9inch) round cake pan.

Sift the flour, sugar, baking powder, bicarbonate of soda and salt into a large bowl.

In a separate bowl, whisk together the milk, oil, cider vinegar, lemon zest and juice, and vanilla extract. Combine the wet and dry ingredients, stirring until smooth.

Pour the batter into the prepared cake pan and bake for 25 minutes, or until a toothpick inserted into the centre of the cakes comes out clean. Remove the cake from the pan and let it cool on a wire rack.

To make the syrup, put all the milk syrup ingredients in a pan and gently simmer for 5 minutes. Turn off the heat and let it steep for at least an hour, then strain.

When everything is cooled, poke some small holes in your cake and pour the milk syrup over. Let it soak into the sponge.

Whip together the cream and icing sugar until it forms stiff peaks. Top the cake with the freshly whipped cream and decorate with chopped strawberries.

Light a sage green or purple candle while you enjoy the calming properties of the chamomile in this delicious milk cake.

LISTENING TO OURSELVES IS AN ART WE PRACTISE LESS AND LESS. THE CONNECTION BETWEEN MIND, BODY AND SOUL HAS GRADUALLY BECOME DISMANTLED. WHAT IF THE HEIGHTENED STATE OF AWARENESS DURING DIFFERENT PHASES OF THE MENSTRUAL CYCLE WERE NOT SOME UNWANTED HYSTERIA THAT SHOULD BE MEDICATED? WHAT IF INSTEAD WE COULD WORK WITH THAT ENERGY TO HARNESS IT AND TAP INTO SOME ANIMALISTIC INTUITION OFTEN HIDDEN BY THE RHYTHMS OF MODERN LIFE? LISTENING ISN'T ALWAYS EASY – BUT IT'S AMAZING WHAT YOU CAN HEAR WHEN YOU TUNE IN TO YOURSELF.

BROOMSTICK BREWS

FROM CEREMONIAL COFFEE TO ALCOHOL ALCHEMY

Rituals play a powerful role in our lives, even when we don't realise it. A perfect example is the Roman Baths in the city of Bath, where visitors once tossed coins into a wishing well, linking the act of throwing a coin to the magic of making a wish. However, when the Baths switched to a cashless system during the pandemic, donations dropped by £90,000 ($115,000) a year. Why? Because tapping a card lacked the ceremony of tossing a coin into water. That physical act made the wish feel real, proving that rituals – whether we believe in them or not – make our intentions more tangible.

In the same way, preparing a recipe or a drink can be transformed into a ritual. It's not just about the magical properties of the ingredients, but also the intention and mindfulness you bring to each step. The simple act of brewing a tea, pouring a coffee or blending a magical moon milk potion can be a way to focus your energy and align your intentions with the natural properties of the herbs you're using. Ingredients like lemon balm, coffee or mint are more than flavours; they carry symbolic meanings and energies that enhance your purpose, whether it's for relaxation, protection or clarity.

WITCH BOTTLE SWEET VERMOUTH

Witch bottles are common in British folk magic and were used as apotropaic charms for protection against witchcraft. Historically, fear of curses was widespread, and cunning folk sold protective charms and spells to combat the superstition. Witch bottles typically contained items such as written charms, hair, urine, pins, needles, wine and rosemary. The pins captured evil, the wine drowned it, and rosemary banished it. Much like the Nazar amulet which offers protection from the evil eye, witch bottles trapped negative energy. These bottles remain iconic symbols of folk magic practices today.

Wormwood, a powerful herb, was often used to ensure no ill will escaped the bottle. Wormwood's common use is more recognizable by its Latin name, *Artemisia absinthium* – wormwood is the main ingredient in absinthe. Famously dubbed 'the green fairy', absinthe has a reputation for creating mind-altering states and is known for its traditional ritual of preparation using a sugar cube soaked in alcohol which is then set alight. Instead, we use wormwood in here to remove any negative energy trapped in the bottle of this powerful protection recipe.

MAKES APPROXIMATELY 1 LITRE (1 QUART)

1 tsp dried wormwood
1 tsp dried chamomile
3 cinnamon sticks
12 dried juniper berries
1 strip of orange peel
1 strip of lemon peel
1 tsp dried fennel seeds
1 star anise
1 vanilla pod (bean)
1 x 75cl (750ml) bottle light white wine
240ml (1 cup) cream sherry

To bind the protection to yourself, carve your initials into the fresh orange and lemon peel.

Add all the ingredients apart from the sherry to a saucepan and bring to the boil. Boil for no longer than a couple of minutes, then remove from the heat and allow to cool. Add the sherry and leave in a cool dark place to infuse overnight.

The following day, strain the liquid through a cheesecloth or fine mesh strainer. Pour into a sterile bottle and store in the fridge or a cool dark place – perhaps in the farthest corner of your home from the front door or under the hearth, as is traditional in folk magic! Once prepared, you can use this vermouth in Negronis, Manhattans or simply on the rocks. Don't forget to toast your enemies and their ill wishes – now turned to power and positivity!

WORMWOOD HAS ASSOCIATIONS WITH PROTECTION, BINDING AND ATTRACTING LOVE. ITS HISTORICAL USE IN ABSINTHE ALSO IMBUES IT WITH TRANSFORMATIVE SYMBOLISM, MAKING IT PERFECT FOR TURNING NEGATIVITY INTO LOVE AND PERSONAL POWER.

HAWTHORN BLOODY MARY

Traditionally used for heart tonics and, curiously, as a protection from lightning, hawthorn flowers were used in garlands and wreaths, particularly on May Day. It's best advised, however, never to use these inside the home as hawthorn smells of death and rotting flesh as it decays. I know that doesn't sound particularly appealing, but the hawthorn is a magical and medicinal all-round marvel. For this reason, haw berries traditionally represent death and rebirth. Use this Bloody Mary to toast those you have lost and pay homage to the endless cycle of life and death.

MAKES ABOUT 250ML (1 CUP) OF HAW BERRY SAUCE (ENOUGH FOR 12–15 BLOODY MARYS)

FOR THE HAW BERRY SAUCE:
100g (3½oz) fresh hawthorn berries
1 apple, peeled, cored and chopped into roughly 2.5cm (1 inch) cubes
A chopped nub of fresh horseradish (optional, for extra kick)
60ml (¼ cup) apple cider vinegar
2 dried chillies
1 tbsp sliced fresh ginger
1 cinnamon stick
1 tbsp molasses
2 tsp black pepper
½ tsp ground cinnamon
½ tsp ground allspice
½ tsp celery salt
½ tsp garlic powder
½ tsp mustard powder
A pinch of ground cardamom
A pinch of ground nutmeg
2 tbsp soy sauce
60ml (¼ cup) red wine vinegar

TO MAKE THE BLOODY MARY

SERVES 1
240ml (1 cup) tomato juice
60ml (¼ cup) vodka
2 tbsp Haw Berry Sauce (see above)
1 tbsp lemon juice
A few dashes of hot sauce (adjust to your spice preference)
A splash of pickle brine (optional)

TO GARNISH:
Celery stalk
Lemon wedge
Cornichon pickles

YOU WILL ALSO NEED:
Cocktail shaker
Ice cubes

Add your washed berries, apple and horseradish to a saucepan along with the vinegar, chillies, ginger, cinnamon stick and 60ml (¼ cup) water. Simmer for around 30 minutes – you'll know it's ready as the skins of the haw berries will burst. Once the fruit is softened, remove from the heat. Pour into a fine-mesh sieve and pick out and discard the horseradish, chillies, ginger and cinnamon stick. Mush your fruit through the sieve into a clean pan to get as much pulp as possible whilst leaving behind all the skins and, importantly, the poisonous seeds.

Return this pulp to the heat and add all the remaining ingredients except the vinegar, then simmer until syrupy. Take off the heat and add a little of the red wine vinegar at a time while stirring, until you reach a thick, smooth consistency. Store in a sterile bottle or jar. This sauce will last for up to 8 weeks in the fridge and can be used as a dip, an addition to sauces or for the hot sauce base of a Bloody Mary.

To make the drink, add the tomato juice, vodka, haw berry sauce, lemon juice and hot sauce to a shaker with a few ice cubes. Add a splash of pickle brine if you want an extra layer of complexity. Give it a vigorous shake. Pour over ice in a tall glass. Garnish with a fresh celery stalk, lemon wedge and pickles to add a bit of flair. Serve in the presence of an object or photograph that represents someone you have lost and make a toast in their honour.

IN ANCIENT GREECE, CELERY WAS ASSOCIATED WITH THE UNDERWORLD AND USED IN FUNERALS TO REPRESENT MOURNING AND LIFE'S FLEETING NATURE. YET, CELERY ALSO CROWNED VICTORS IN THE NEMEAN GAMES. THIS CONTRAST REFLECTS THE BELIEF THAT LIFE AND DEATH ARE INTERTWINED, WITH CELERY EMBODYING BOTH THE HONOUR OF THE DECEASED AND THE GLORY OF VICTORY.

THE LEAVES, FLOWERS AND BERRIES OF HAWTHORN, A PROLIFIC COUNTRYSIDE HEDGEROW STAPLE, ARE ALL EDIBLE, BUT IT SHOULD BE NOTED THAT THE SEEDS, LIKE APPLE SEEDS, CONTAIN CYANIDE, SO IT'S VERY IMPORTANT NOT TO INGEST THE SEEDS.

CARMELITE WATER CORDIAL

Carmelite water gets its name from the Carmelite nuns of St Just, who originally crafted it as an alcoholic extract of lemon balm and other herbs. It was then popularized as a herbal health tonic called Eau de Mélisse (after the Latin name for lemon balm, *Melissa officinalis*). Eau de Mélisse can still be purchased today as a cure for nausea, motion sickness, migraines and even as a topical ointment for cuts and bruises. Lemon balm is a mood boosting plant that aids with sleep and reducing stress. It can relieve headaches, inflammation, anxiety and even menstrual cramps. In spell work, lemon balm represents calm, focus, feminine energy, emotional healing and intuition. It's often used in spells to calm anxiety and process trauma alongside therapy and medical intervention. Although traditional recipes call for a great number of herbs, this cordial focuses on the power of the lemon balm. The number of leaves used in this recipe, however, is signifcant as in numerology the number 33 symbolizes creativity and balance.

MAKES 10–15 SERVINGS

200g (1 cup) granulated sugar
240ml (1 cup) water
33 fresh lemon balm leaves, chopped (or 2 tbsp dried)
1 tbsp finely grated lemon zest,
Soda water, to serve
Lime wedges, to serve

Put all the ingredients in a saucepan and bring to a simmer for 5 minutes, stir to dissolve the sugar, then take off the heat. Allow to cool and steep overnight. Strain and pour into a clean bottle or jar. This syrup will keep in the fridge for 2–4 weeks if stored in an airtight container and you strain out the leaves and zest effectively.

To serve, pour a dash of cordial into your glass, over ice, then fill up the glass with soda. Stir, taste and add more cordial if desired. Garnish with a lime wedge.

Alternatively, add the cordial to hot water to consume before bed to get a restful night of sleep or whenever you need a moment of calm.

THE EARLIEST KNOWN RECIPE FOR CARMELITE WATER IS OVER 600 YEARS OLD!

DANDELION AND BURDOCK ROOT BEER

The dandelion symbolizes wishes, time and divination, with its three stages: in flower (the sun), in seed (the moon), and as seeds blow away (the stars). People use dandelion seeds for wish-making, believing they carry fairy spirits. Folklore also claims that the remaining seeds predict years left to live, and blowing seeds toward someone sends a message. Dandelion roots were used as a coffee substitute during the Second World War, while the bitter leaves add zest to salads. Its flowers were made into wine, giving rise to its nickname 'Piss the Bed' due to their diuretic effect.

MAKES APPROXIMATELY 1.5 LITRES (52FL OZ OR 3 BOTTLES)

FOR THE GINGER ROOT CULTURE:
175ml (¾ cup) filtered/boiled water
140ml (9½ tbsp) maple syrup
7 tbsp grated ginger

FOR THE ROOT BEER:
2 tbsp dried sarsaparilla root
2 tbsp dried burdock root
1 tbsp dried liquorice root
1 tbsp dried dandelion root
3 tbsp dandelion petals (fresh or dried)
1 cinnamon stick
100g (½ cup) brown sugar
100ml (scant ½ cup) molasses

To make the ginger root culture, combine the filtered water and 50ml (3½ tablespoons) of the maple syrup in a clean and sterile glass jar. Add 1 tablespoon of grated or chopped ginger root and cover loosely with a cloth. The following day, add 1 tablespoon of both maple syrup and grated ginger to the jar and stir gently. Repeat every day for the following 6 days. Once bubbly, it's ready to be used in your root beer.

To make the root beer, add all of your dried roots, dandelion petals and cinnamon stick to a saucepan along with 1 litre (4¼ cups) of water. Bring the liquid to a boil, then simmer for 20 minutes. Take the pan off the heat and let it steep for at least 2 hours.

Strain the liquid, then pour it into a large glass jar, along with another litre (4¼ cups) of water. Once cool add the ginger root culture, the molasses and sugar. Cover the top with a cloth and store it in a cool dark place. Give it a stir with a wooden spoon three times a day for 3 days.

Strain once more and bottle in sterilized bottles making sure to leave some room at the top for a fizzy head when the bottle is popped. Bottles left too long (4 weeks or more) or not stored properly can explode so make sure you don't forget about it!

BURDOCK ROOTS WERE SAID TO BE BEST GATHERED AROUND THE WANING MOON AND WERE WORN FOR HEALING AND PROTECTION.

FOUR CAULDRON COFFEE SYRUPS

A coffee spell has become part of an everyday practice for me. It's the easiest way to focus my day and sow a little magic into the mundane inertia of daily life. It's not always accessible or practical to be baking up spells from scratch or foraging in the wilderness – but even the stirring of your coffee can be a small ceremony to bring mindful ritual into your daily life. Personally, I love a mocha pot. Living on a boat has meant that I do not have access to the convenience of unlimited electricity, so I got used to relying on gas (and the stack stove above my fire in winter) for all my cooking. However, even if you're using a kettle, a cafetière, or even a coffee machine, you can still add these syrups and bring a little spell into your morning routine.

VANILLA AND CARDAMON SYRUP

FOR CONFIDENCE

This classic syrup adds a sweet, smooth vanilla flavour with an edge of floral spice. Both vanilla and cardamon promote feelings of love and mental clarity. Perfect for when you need a confidence boost.

MAKES 10–15 SERVINGS

200g (1 cup) sugar (use white or brown sugar, depending on preference)
5 whole cardamom pods
4 vanilla pods (beans), cut lengthways

YOU WILL ALSO NEED:
A yellow or orange candle (optional)

In a small saucepan, combine the sugar, cardamom pods and vanilla pods with 240ml (1 cup) water over medium heat. Stir occasionally (clockwise) until the sugar is fully dissolved. Once the sugar is dissolved, remove from heat and allow the syrup cool completely.

Take out the vanilla and cardamon pods and transfer the syrup to a bottle or jar. Store in the fridge for up to 2 weeks, and use to sweeten your coffee and add a rich and confident vanilla note. You can light a yellow or orange candle and stir your coffee clockwise to 'bring in' the confidence when you drink it, if you want to add extra potency to the ritual!

ORANGE SYRUP

FOR CREATIVE ENERGY

The colour orange has strong associations with creativity. Orange flavours also promote concentration, confidence and provide a dash of luck. I love it in an espresso, but it's also great in a mocha.

MAKES 10–15 SERVINGS

200g (1 cup) sugar
Zest of 1 orange, pared into strips

YOU WILL ALSO NEED:
An orange candle (optional)

In a saucepan, combine the sugar and orange zest with 240ml (1 cup) water. Stir until the sugar is dissolved, then simmer for 5 minutes to infuse the zest. Remove from heat and leave to cool.

Strain the syrup and pour into a bottle. Store in the fridge for up to 2 weeks. This adds a lovely citrus brightness to coffee drinks. When adding it into your morning coffee ritual you might want to light an orange candle and stir it clockwise to bring in creativity and focus.

GINGER, CINNAMON AND BROWN SUGAR SYRUP

FOR FINANCIAL SUCCESS

A zesty, warming syrup with a touch of spice, perfect for adding a zing to your coffee and success to your day! Ginger is known for manifesting prosperity and producing positive results. Cinnamon is connected with wealth and abundance. Use this coffee syrup when you want to add some prosperity into your day.

MAKES 10–15 SERVINGS

200g (1 cup) brown sugar
2 cinnamon sticks
2 tbsp finely chopped or grated fresh ginger

YOU WILL ALSO NEED:
A green candle (optional)

In a saucepan, combine the sugar, cinnamon and ginger with 240ml (1 cup) water. Bring to a simmer over medium heat, stirring clockwise until the sugar dissolves. Let it simmer for 10 minutes to infuse the ginger and cinnamon flavours, then remove from the heat and let it cool.

Strain out the ginger and cinnamon pieces and pour the syrup into a bottle. Store in the fridge for up to 2 weeks and add to your coffee according to taste. You can light a green candle and stir your coffee clockwise to 'bring in' the prosperity as you drink.

MINT SYRUP

FOR HEALING AND PROTECTION

A refreshing and minty syrup, perfect for making a mint mocha or hot chocolate at home – mint has strong associations with healing and protection, so use this whenever you are in need of an extra boost of reassurance and care.

MAKES 10–15 SERVINGS

200g (1 cup) sugar
10–15 mint leaves, chopped

YOU WILL ALSO NEED:
A white candle (optional)

In a saucepan, combine the sugar with 240ml (1 cup) water and set over medium heat, stirring until the sugar is dissolved. Remove from the heat, add your mint leaves and leave to cool. Once cool, strain and pour into a bottle and store in the fridge for up to 2 weeks.

Use this coffee ritual on days when you want to feel protected. If you specifically want to banish negativity, you can add a little pinch of black pepper when you make your coffee. Light a white candle as you drink and focus on your intentions.

COFFEE HAS DEEP TIES TO MAGIC AND MYSTICISM. IN BOTH ETHIOPIA AND YEMEN, IT WAS BELIEVED TO HAVE POWERFUL SPIRITUAL PROPERTIES AND FOLKLORIC STORIES OF ORIGIN. IN SUFI MONASTERIES, COFFEE WAS USED TO AID RELIGIOUS DEVOTION, WHILE IN ETHIOPIA, IT WAS OFTEN LINKED TO RITUALS AND ENERGY-BOOSTING PRACTICES. COFFEE'S USE AS A SPIRITUAL TOOL EXTENDED INTO ISLAMIC CULTURE, WHERE IT WAS REVERED FOR ITS ABILITY TO ENHANCE FOCUS DURING PRAYER.

MOON MILK

Here you will find a collection of my go-to moon milks, simple milk infusions which I use to manifest different goals and mindsets into my life. Enjoy at any time of day, whenever you need that extra boost.

LIQUID GOLD TURMERIC AND SAFFRON MOON MILK

TO ATTRACT WEALTH

This moon milk helps you to tap into a frequency of mindfulness that invites money into your life. I like to use oat milk for this one as oats have an abundance of great nutritional qualities and also represent reaping the harvest.

SERVES 1

- **300ml (1¼ cups) milk of your choice**
- **1 tsp ground turmeric**
- **⅓ tsp ground cinnamon**
- **½ tsp ground ginger**
- **A tiny pinch of sea salt and black pepper**
- **1 tbsp maple syrup**
- **1 slice of lemon peel**
- **A few strands of saffron**
- **1 bay leaf**

YOU WILL ALSO NEED:
A yellow candle

Firstly, light the candle to open the circle.

In a saucepan, gently heat your milk. Add the spices, maple syrup and lemon peel. Using a pestle and mortar, gently bash the saffron strands before adding 3 tablespoons of hot water to them (if you don't have one, add the water to the strands as they are). Pour this liquid into your moon milk.

On your bay leaf, write what you would like to manifest, whether this be a salary increase at work or something more ambiguous like 'money'. Add this to your milk and stir clockwise seven times.

Strain into a cup and drink while focusing on what you want to manifest. When you are finished, blow out the candle to close the circle.

LOVE SPELL MOON MILK

TO MANIFEST LOVE

Cardamon, rose and apple are all heavily associated with love, while the chilli, ginger and cinnamon add warmth and energy to this brew. This moon milk is designed to attract love into your life, and to strengthen self-love.

SERVES 1

300ml (1¼ cups) milk of your choice
1 tbsp dried rose petals
1 tsp ground cardamon
3 cardamon pods
½ tsp ground cinnamon
1 tsp chilli flakes
½ tsp ground ginger
1 tbsp maple syrup
1 apple

YOU WILL ALSO NEED:
A pink candle

Firstly, light the candle to open the circle.

In a saucepan, gently heat your milk. Add all the remaining ingredients except the apple. Stir clockwise seven times. Strain and pour into a cup, and drink while focusing on the love you wish to manifest. Slice and eat the apple.

When you are finished, blow out the candle to close the circle.

SUNSHINE IN A MUG MORNING MOON MILK

TO MANIFEST JOY AND CONFIDENCE

Marigolds invite admiration, joy and justice into your life. This is the perfect start to big important days when you need a boost of confidence and energy. As well as an energy and mood booster, this spell is especially effective for official and legal matters – think job interviews, business meetings and even days in court – as long as you are on the side of justice, marigold will back you.

SERVES 1

300ml (1¼ cups) milk of your choice
½ tsp ground turmeric
2 tbsp dried calendula (marigold)
Grated zest of 1 orange
1 tbsp maple syrup

YOU WILL ALSO NEED:
1 orange or yellow candle

Light the candle to open the circle.

In a saucepan, gently heat your milk along with all the other ingredients. Stir clockwise seven times. Strain and pour into a cup, and drink while focusing on your intentions!

When you are finished, blow out the candle to close the circle.

OFTEN ASSOCIATED WITH PROTECTION AND HEALING, MARIGOLD WAS USED IN MEDIEVAL BRITISH MEDICINE FOR ITS ANTI-INFLAMMATORY PROPERTIES. IT WAS ALSO THOUGHT TO PROTECT HOMES AND GARDENS FROM EVIL.

LAVENDER AND CBD SLEEPY MOON MILK

TO CURB ANXIETY

This is the perfect milk to add into your nightly routine for a calm night's sleep. Taking a few moments of ritualistic calm to ensure you get a quality night's sleep will be more beneficial than any skincare routine – trust me.

SERVES 1

300ml (1¼ cups) milk of your choice
1 tbsp dried lavender
1 tbsp dried lemon balm
3 drops of food-grade CBD oil
A tiny pinch of salt and black pepper
1 tbsp maple syrup

YOU WILL ALSO NEED:
A blue candle

Light the candle to open the circle.

In a saucepan, gently heat all the ingredients. Stir clockwise seven times while focusing on calming relaxation. Strain into a mug and curl up with a book somewhere cozy.

When you are finished, blow out the candle to close the circle and go to bed without any screens or distractions.

You can also write your worries out on a piece of paper while you drink this milk and put it under your pillow for your dreams to carry away. You should feel less anxious about what's troubling you by morning.

PRACTICAL MAGIC

FULL RITUAL RECIPE SPELLS

This chapter delves into incorporating more detailed ritual elements to recipes to create intentional change. It emphasizes the power of aligning your actions with the phases of the moon, and using simple tools like candles, incense, crystals and spoken affirmations. These elements add depth and potency to rituals aimed at addressing common challenges, such as improving self-confidence, managing finances or reducing anxiety.

Rather than being overly complex, the rituals in this chapter provide a framework to enhance ordinary actions with purpose and symbolism – using ingredients more commonly found in the average store cupboard than the foraged plants used in most of the previous chapters. These recipe spells and rituals guide you in transforming daily routines into magical acts, turning something as innocuous as preparing a meal or making breakfast into opportunities to align with your goals. This chapter seeks to embed everything you have learned throughout *Kitchen Magic* into a higher level of ritual recipe work that is not difficult – but that engages multiple elements for added efficacy. It demonstrates that even small, thoughtful acts can create powerful ripple effects.

RECOMMENDATIONS

I have made recommendations for the days of the week and moon phases when your recipe spell will be most potent to perform, as well as candle, crystal and incense suggestions. Each of these 'ingredients' will add strength to your intention but you do not need to stick rigidly to these suggestions – spells, just like recipes, are adaptable. Before beginning each ritual spell in this chapter, light your suggested candle and incense to open the circle. Remember to stir clockwise to 'bring in' your intention or anticlockwise to cast something away. You may choose to meditate on your crystal or hold it while speaking your incantation if you decide to use one. And finally, recite the incantation with gusto – even if it feels silly – laugh it, shout it, sing it! You are making a promise aloud, so it needs to be heard!

THE SPOKEN WORD

One of the most powerful – but simple – aspects of spell work we can incorporate is the spoken word. For example, the Greeks, like many other ancient civilizations, did not have a specific word for the colour blue. This absence wasn't just linguistic – it shaped their very perception of colour itself – they did not distinguish blue as a separate colour but instead as a hue of green or grey. Modern research has shown that language and culture deeply influence how we see the world. Without a word for a particular hue, like blue, it becomes more challenging for people to identify or distinguish it. This means our understanding of colour is guided not only by biology, but by cultural and linguistic contexts. The Egyptians, who did have a word for blue, were one of the few ancient cultures to recognize and describe the colour, likely due to their invention of blue dye.

This connection between language and perception is reflected in the power of words themselves, particularly when it comes to magic and rituals. The word 'spell' in the context of magic originates from the Old English word 'spel', meaning speech or story. A spell, then, is essentially spoken word imbued with intent and power, much like the act of spelling out words. Folk magic traditions emphasized the importance of vocalized incantations and charms. These incantations weren't just idle words but carefully constructed phrases believed to have tangible effects on the physical world.

This belief in the power of spoken words persists today. Affirmations, for example, harness the energy of language to shape our mindset and reality. In magical practice, the spoken word is seen as a bridge between intention and manifestation. When we vocalize a spell, chant or affirmation, we're engaging in a form of symbolic creation, giving our thoughts and desires shape and form through sound. Whether it's a folk charm, a prayer or a modern affirmation, the act of speaking allows us to direct energy and intention outward into the universe, reinforcing the idea that words are not just communicative – they are transformative.

Spells are themselves recipes – each ingredient, such as a moon phase, crystal or colour, can enhance the power of the ritual. Although it is not necessary to stick rigidly to every single aspect of the spell, and substitutions can be made (again, much like a cooking recipe) each piece of the puzzle adds potency to the pot.

MAPLE AND VANILLA MARINATED TOMATO SALAD

A LOVE SPELL

Basil, often called a 'witch's herb', has a fascinating and divisive history. The Greeks believed one must insult basil for it to thrive, and in French, 'sow basil' still means to rant. In Italy, where basil is known as the 'herb of love', giving a pot of basil to a lover was a sign of deep affection, and it was often placed on balconies or windowsills by women to signal their readiness for courtship. It symbolizes love, prosperity and protection across many cultures. Similarly, the tomato, or 'pomme d'amour' ('love apple'), was once believed to be an aphrodisiac, further associating it with love and passion due to its heart-like shape and vibrant colour.

MOON PHASE: WAXING MOON – **to draw in new beginnings and love.**

DAY OF THE WEEK: FRIDAY – **ruled by Venus, perfect for love and attraction spells.**

CANDLE COLOUR: PINK – **associated with affection, romance and emotional connections.**

INCENSE: JASMINE – **enhances love and attraction.**

CRYSTAL: ROSE QUARTZ – **promotes unconditional love and draws romantic energy.**

SERVES 4–6 (AS A SIDE DISH)

6 tomatoes
1 tsp vanilla bean paste
1 tbsp maple syrup
10 basil leaves (various sizes)
Sea salt and black pepper

YOU WILL ALSO NEED:
A pink candle
A pen and paper
An appropriate book (see method)

Cut a shallow cross in the top of each of your tomatoes and place them in a bowl of just-boiled water for 1–2 minutes. While they sit, recite this incantation:

With fruit and flower, in moonlight's glow,
Let love's pure essence start to flow.
A kindred spirit, a heart to heart,
Now drawn to me, we'll never part.

The skins should begin to blister. Remove the tomatoes and place in a bowl of cold water for 2 minutes to cool. By now it should be easy to remove the skins.

In the meantime, mix your vanilla paste and maple syrup with 3 tablespoons of water.

Slice your tomatoes and place them flat on a plate. Sprinkle a pinch of salt and pepper on top and drench them with your vanilla mixture. Add your whole basil leaves on top. As you enjoy the sweetness of this recipe, light a pink candle and write a list of 12 traits you would seek in a potential partner.

Save 12 tomato seeds from the dish and place them on the paper. Fold the paper three times and place it inside a book that represents something you would wish to find in a new love – this could be a hobby that relates to the book, or something in the story that speaks to you. Put this book back on your shelf and do not touch it. By the time it is picked up again, you will be in love.

VANILLA WAS HIGHLY PRIZED BY THE AZTECS AND MAYANS, WHO USED IT TO FLAVOUR THEIR CHOCOLATE DRINKS, OFTEN IN CEREMONIAL CONTEXTS. THE VANILLA ORCHID WAS CONSIDERED A SYMBOL OF FERTILITY AND SENSUALITY, LINKING IT TO LOVE AND PASSION. THE AZTECS, IN PARTICULAR, BELIEVED THAT VANILLA HAD APHRODISIACAL PROPERTIES, ENHANCING ROMANTIC AND SENSUAL EXPERIENCES.

RHUBARB AND CARDAMOM CUSTARD TART

A SPELL FOR REIGNITING THE SPARK!

Rhubarb, with its bright crimson stalks, has historically been associated with love, passion and fidelity. Rhubarb has also been linked to sexual energy and is thought to enhance desire and commitment between lovers. Similarly, cardamom has roots in love spells – often used for drawing lovers closer and offering protection to relationships. If you and your lover are seeking to reignite the spark and deepen your commitment, this tart serves as both a delicious dessert and a ritual to rekindle passion and break away from the constraints of perfection. As you share this sweet treat, take the time to nourish your connection – both physically and emotionally. The magic of this tart is in the eating, where each bite is an opportunity to visualize your future together and share things you've never allowed yourself to share before. The rhubarb and custard flavours are reminiscent of childhood innocence, encouraging openness, laughter, play and vulnerability.

MOON PHASE: FULL MOON – amplifies passion and emotional bonds.

DAY OF THE WEEK: FRIDAY – Venus rules passion and relationships.

CANDLE COLOUR: RED – for rekindling passion and desire.

INCENSE: SANDALWOOD – heightens sensuality and intimacy.

CRYSTAL: GARNET – revitalizes love and rekindles connection.

SERVES 6–8

1 sheet of ready-rolled shortcrust pastry

FOR THE CUSTARD:
500ml (2 cups) milk of your choice
100g (½ cup) caster (superfine) sugar
4 tbsp cornflour (cornstarch)
1 tsp vanilla extract
1 tsp ground cardamom
1 cardamom pod

FOR THE RHUBARB TOPPING:
3–4 rhubarb stalks, cut into lengths
2 tbsp caster (superfine) sugar
Finely grated zest of 1 orange

Ideally this one should be cooked together with your lover. Start by preheating your oven to 180°C/350°F/Gas 4.

Use the ready-rolled shortcrust pastry to line a 23-cm (9 inch) tart pan, pressing it gently into the edges. Trim any excess pastry around the edge and prick the base with a fork. Line the pastry case with a sheet of baking parchment and fill with rice or baking beans. Blind bake the pastry for 10–15 minutes until the edges are golden. Remove the baking beans or rice and bake for a further couple of minutes to slightly brown the base.

While the pastry is in the oven, prepare the rhubarb. Place the stalks in a large wide pan - you want the stalks to be as long as possible – with the sugar, orange zest and 1 tablespoon water. Simmer the stalks for a couple of minutes until slightly tender but still holding their shape. Leave to cool.

In another saucepan, gently heat the milk with the sugar, cornflour, vanilla and both types of cardamom, whisking continuously until the mixture thickens into a creamy custard. Leave the single cardamon pod in the custard.

Once the pastry has cooled slightly, pour in the custard and place the tart in the fridge for 2 hours to allow it to set. While the tart cools, take a moment to each write down something you've never had the courage to share with your partner before. This could be something you've always wanted to tell them, something vulnerable you want them to know, or simply a compliment you've been too bashful to let them know.

RECIPE CONTINUES OVERLEAF

Once the custard has set, weave the rhubarb stalks together on top of the tart to represent the intertwining of your lives. This is quite a fiddly task, but the lesson is that nothing is perfect. Work together, laugh together – and remember that we are not striving for perfection. While doing so, recite the following incantation in unison:

As rhubarb weaves this pie anew,
Let love's sweet bond weave stronger too.
Hearts align, leave behind perfection.
Instead, the simple joy of our connection.

When the tart is ready to serve, feed your lover the first bite while locking eyes, focusing on the renewed spark and energy flowing between you. Enjoy the moment, savour the sweet flavours, and let this shared ritual bring you closer. Whoever bites the cardamon pod is invited to share aloud their written note first.

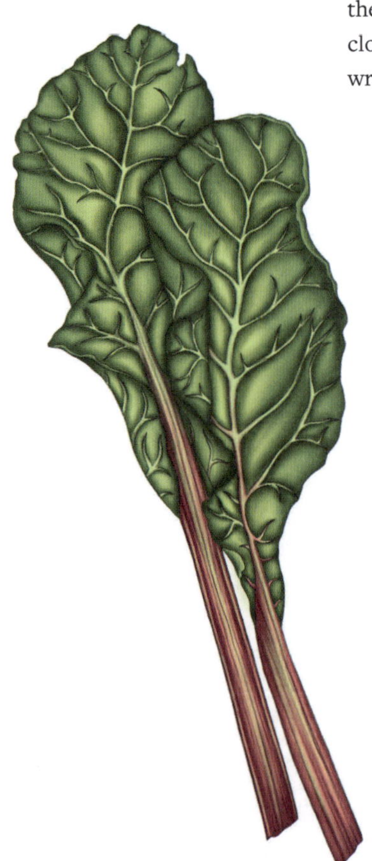

ROSE AND BASIL TURKISH DELIGHT

A SPELL FOR SETTING BOUNDARIES (WITH LOVE)

Basil and rose are powerful symbols of protection and love, making them ideal ingredients for a ritual focused on setting boundaries – but with kindness. Roses, with their delicate beauty, are symbolic of love and care, but their thorns serve as a reminder of the need for protective boundaries and personal space. This Turkish delight ritual embodies the balance between setting boundaries – whether with yourself or others – while remaining an act of love. While the protective energy of each ingredient affirms your space, the loving properties serve as a gentle reminder that boundaries are not just about separation but also about self-respect and maintaining healthy, loving relationships. As you share or consume these sweet treats, the process becomes a meditative act of establishing your space – whether you wish to keep someone at a distance, or to honour your own personal boundaries.

MOON PHASE: WANING MOON – to release negative dynamics and set boundaries.

DAY OF THE WEEK: SATURDAY – ruled by Saturn, great for structure and boundaries.

CANDLE COLOUR: WHITE – purity and clarity for setting intentions.

INCENSE: ROSE – balances love with harmony.

CRYSTAL: AMETHYST – supports emotional clarity and healthy boundaries.

MAKES 9–12 CUBES

22 fresh basil leaves
400g (2 cups) caster (superfine) sugar
1 tbsp lemon juice
100g (1 cup) cornflour (cornstarch), plus 1 tbsp extra for dusting
1 tsp cream of tartar
1 tbsp rosewater or a few drops of rose extract
Neutral oil, for greasing (optional)
2 tbsp icing (powdered) sugar
1 dried rose petal

YOU WILL ALSO NEED:
A pen and paper

Begin by placing the 22 fresh basil leaves (22 representing order, structure and manifestation in numerology) in 500ml (2 cups) cold water and refrigerate for 2 hours. As the basil infuses, take time to write down the boundaries you wish to set, focusing on how they will protect your space while maintaining love and care for yourself or others. When the water is ready, strain out the basil.

In a saucepan, heat the infused water, sugar and lemon juice, stirring until the sugar dissolves.

Mix the cornflour, cream of tartar, and a splash of water to form a smooth paste, then slowly stir this into the sugar mixture. Continue to cook while whisking gently until the mixture becomes thick and jelly-like. Add the rosewater or rose extract, imagining the love and protection the rose represents as you stir it in.

Grease or line a 20 x 20-cm (8 x 8-inch) baking tin or dish with baking parchment. Once the mixture is ready, pour it into the prepared tin or dish. Place a single rose petal into the middle and let it cool slightly before putting in the fridge overnight to set.

On a plate, combine the icing sugar with the 1 tablespoon of cornflour for dusting. When the Turkish delight is firm, cut it into small cubes (making sure one of them has the rose petal suspended inside) and toss them in the sugar and cornflour. Each piece represents a boundary you are setting, infused with love and respect. Take the piece with the rose petal and repeat this incantation before eating it:

RECIPE CONTINUES OVERLEAF

With rose's grace and basil's might,
I claim my space, yet hearts stay light.
Boundaries bloom where love may grow,
Respect and peace, this spell bestow.

If you are setting boundaries with someone in your life, consider gifting or sharing the Turkish delight with them. If your boundaries are for yourself or someone you wish to permanently distance from, enjoy the treat alone.

If kept in the fridge, your Turkish delight will last up to a month. Keep in an airtight box or jar with the paper of your written intentions underneath the Turkish delight. Each time you take a piece to enjoy with some hot tea, remember that you are solidifying your boundaries. When the sweets are finished, burn the paper and scatter the ashes in the four corners of your room or home, sealing your intentions in place.

SYMPATHETIC MAGIC IS A FORM OF SPELL, CHARM OR RITUAL THAT TIES TO A PERSON (INCLUDING YOURSELF) USING AN OBJECT. THIS MIGHT BE SOMETHING RELATING TO THEM (SUCH AS THEIR NAME OR A PHOTOGRAPH), SOMETHING FROM THEIR PERSON (SUCH AS A HAIR OR ITEM), OR SOMETHING THAT REPRESENTS THEM (SUCH AS A DOLL). ALTHOUGH IT IS NOT ADVISED TO CAST SPELLS OVER OTHERS WITHOUT THEIR KNOWLEDGE OR CONSENT, IT IS ABSOLUTELY PERMISSIBLE TO DO SPELLS TOGETHER AND FOR/WITH OTHERS IF THEY ARE AWARE. IN KITCHEN WITCHERY, THERE IS NO BETTER WAY TO DO THIS THAN TO COOK TOGETHER OR SHARE THE RECIPE YOU'VE MADE WITH THE PERSON IT'S INTENDED FOR. YOU CAN TIE IT TO THEM WITH A SIGIL OF THEIR NAME OR AN INGREDIENT GIVEN TO YOU BY THEM – BUT I WOULDN'T ADVISE ADDING A HAIR!

HEDGEROW PANCAKES

A MINDFULNESS SPELL

This recipe is not about the ingredients; it's about the process. The act of going out for a walk is an integral part of this dish, so make sure you set an intention to make it on a lazy day. Savour the experience and enjoy connecting yourself to the land around you. This recipe is a challenge – not in the sense that it's difficult or arduous, but in that it's something I am putting to you. For most of the recipes in this book, the foraged or more unusual ingredients can be sourced online or replaced with more accessible counterparts. But for this recipe, I want you to go out and see what you can find around you. Even if you come back empty handed and reach for the bagged spinach or frozen berries – it doesn't matter. The act of mindfully stepping out of your door on a hunt for something to sustain yourself from the land is what's important here. Not every hunt is victorious, but it doesn't mean the process isn't worthy.

MOON PHASE: NEW MOON – for fresh mental clarity and setting intentions.

DAY OF THE WEEK: MONDAY – ruled by the Moon, ideal for introspection (but any day when you don't have much going on will work – chose a day when you don't have any plans).

CANDLE COLOUR: BLUE – encourages calm and mindfulness.

INCENSE: LAVENDER – soothes the mind and promotes inner peace.

CRYSTAL: CLEAR QUARTZ – enhances focus and mental clarity.

MAKES 6–8 THICK PANCAKES

140g (1 cup plus 1 tbsp) plain (all-purpose) flour
2 tbsp sugar (optional, depending if you want sweet or savoury pancakes)
1 tbsp baking powder
⅛ tsp sea salt
240ml (1 cup) milk of your choice
Oil, for cooking
1 tsp vanilla extract (optional)
Chopped foraged findings (such as blackberries and lemon verbena)

Begin by strolling through nature, taking time to notice the plants and wildlife around you. You may want to take your clear quartz and hold it in your pocket to ground yourself as you enjoy being in nature and interacting mindfully with the plants. Once you've foraged confidently (see page 27), return home to a calm cooking space. Open the circle by lighting your candle and incense.

In a bowl, combine the flour, sugar, baking powder and salt. In a separate bowl, combine the milk and oil, and the vanilla if making sweet pancakes. Slowly add the wet ingredients to the dry, whisking to form a smooth batter. Gently fold in your gathered finds and recite this incantation:

With nature's gifts, this batter blends,
A mindful act where calm extends.
Each foraged taste, a moment's care,
Brings balance, joy and love to share.

Heat a drizzle of oil in a large frying pan. Add a ladleful of the batter and fry for a few minutes on each side until golden and browned. As you cook the pancake, remain present, appreciating the sounds, smells and textures as they change. Repeat to cook all the batter, adding a little more oil to the pan for each pancake, then serve the pancakes with gratitude for the land, savouring both the flavours and the mindful adventure that brought you to this moment. Enjoy.

MINDFULNESS HAS BECOME SOMEWHAT OF A BUZZWORD – AND WHILE IT CAN FEEL OVERUSED, IT HAS SUCCESSFULLY BROUGHT A POWERFUL CONCEPT INTO EVERYDAY LIFE. BUT LIKE MEDITATION, IT'S EASIER IN THEORY THAN IN PRACTISE. USING FOLK MEDICINE, PLANT MAGIC AND RITUALS RATHER THAN HABITS TEACHES US TO LISTEN TO OURSELVES, GIVING US INSTRUCTION ON HOW TO STAY MINDFUL AND PRESENT.

ORANGE, SALT AND ROSEMARY OATCAKES

A SPELL FOR CONFIDENCE AND BRAVERY

Oats are a sturdy base for any spell recipe relating to mental/emotional well-being and feeling sure and confident of yourself. They bring energy and calm to the table. Salt is well known as a protective and banishing force – it's powerful and grounding, and keeps harm at bay. The orange adds a dash of optimism and confidence. Rosemary cleanses the body or space of negative energy and instils tranquillity and calm.

MOON PHASE: WAXING MOON – **builds personal power and courage.**

DAY OF THE WEEK: TUESDAY – **ruled by Mars, aligned with bravery and strength.**

CANDLE COLOUR: ORANGE – **ignites confidence and courage.**

INCENSE: CEDAR WOOD – **bolsters inner strength and determination.**

CRYSTAL: CARNELIAN – **energizes courage and self-esteem.**

MAKES 6–8 OATCAKES

160g (1 cup) fine oatmeal
2 tbsp chopped fresh rosemary
1 tsp flaked sea salt
2 tbsp grated orange peel
1 tbsp olive oil
6–8 tbsp moon water (ideally, see page 30, created under the light of a waxing moon)
Plain (all-purpose) flour, for dusting

Begin by gathering your ingredients in a quiet, undisturbed space and opening the circle by lighting your candle.

Preheat the oven to 160°C/320°F/Gas 3 and line a baking tray with baking parchment.

In a bowl, combine the oatmeal, rosemary, salt and orange peel, stirring them together gently while visualizing your intentions infusing each element. As you add the olive oil, imagine it as a protective barrier, sealing in your positive energy.

Next, gradually mix in the moon water, envisioning it as a flow of confidence and calmness that binds your mixture together. As you knead the dough into a sticky yet sturdy consistency, repeat this incantation:

With orange zest and rosemary power,
Salt clears my path in this bold hour.
Confidence grows as I take my stand,
Strong and steady, heart in hand.

Roll out your dough on a floured surface until it is about 1cm (½ inch) thick. Cut out your oatcakes with the mouth of a 10–13cm (4–5 inch) wide mug or glass, or a cookie cutter of the same size. Place them on the prepared baking tray and bake for 25 minutes until slightly browned on top, filling your home with the aroma of optimism and confidence.

Once baked, let the oatcakes cool and take a moment to meditate on the strength they represent. Store them in a sealed container with a photograph of yourself to tie your energy to the intention. Each time you enjoy one, repeat the incantation and reflect on your journey toward confidence and bravery, grounding your intentions in each bite. These oatcakes will keep for 3–4 days in an airtight container.

DAILY ABUNDANCE PORRIDGE

A MONEY SPELL

Incorporating simple rituals into your daily routine can unlock the power of intention. A mindful breakfast, such as porridge, can set the tone for your day while helping you stay aligned with your goals. Whether manifesting abundance or managing spending, preparing and eating porridge with focus can transform this everyday meal into a daily act of commitment. While habits can feel rigid, rituals allow flexibility, adapting to how you feel in the moment while still maintaining purpose. Instead of a vague habit such as 'save more money', a ritual – like adding to a money bowl daily – makes your goal tangible and reinforces it. Rituals help shape the habits you want, transforming abstract goals into intentional, regular actions.

MOON PHASE: **Any time, but you can use moon water created under a waxing moon to draw abundance and prosperity.**

DAY OF THE WEEK: **This spell is designed with consistency in mind (doing it every day for a period of time), but it will be especially potent on a Thursday as it is ruled by Jupiter, associated with wealth and luck – I recommend starting or finishing several days of this spell on a Thursday.**

CANDLE COLOUR: GREEN – **symbolizes growth and financial success.**

INCENSE: PATCHOULI – **attracts prosperity and wealth.**

CRYSTAL: CITRINE – **energizes abundance and attracts financial opportunities.**

SERVES 1

60g (2/3 cup) oats
120ml (½ cup) milk of your choice (or water)
A pinch of ground cinnamon
1 small apple, half grated and half sliced
1 tbsp maple syrup
1 tbsp nut butter
A pinch of sea salt

Start by lighting your candle and incense, while focusing on your financial intentions. Cook the oats in milk (or water) in a saucepan over a gentle heat, stirring clockwise to visualize prosperity flowing into your life. Add cinnamon for wealth, grated apple to sweeten your path, and a spoon of nut butter for stability. Season with a pinch of salt for protection, a drizzle of maple syrup for sweetness and top with apple slices for growth. Before you tuck in, recite these words:

With cinnamon's warmth and mindful ways,
Abundance grows through steady days.
This daily bowl, with care inhabits,
The power held in rituals, not habits.

As you eat, savour each bite with mindful intention, visualizing your goals becoming reality. Once finished, write down three financial goals – daily, monthly and yearly. This could be a savings target or a manifestation. It doesn't matter if these repeat each time you write them – they should ideally be consistent. When finished, extinguish the candle with gratitude, reinforcing your commitment to financial abundance. The method behind this ritual is not elaborate ceremony to be performed once and forgotten about – this is about consistency. Repeat daily or at least once per week to stay connected to your goals.

UNLIKE HABITS, WHICH STRUGGLE IN A FLUCTUATING WORLD, RITUALS PROVIDE A CUE TO FOCUS. THEY INTERRUPT AUTOPILOT PATTERNS AND ANCHOR YOUR THOUGHTS, HELPING YOU STAY GROUNDED AND PURPOSEFUL. BY INCORPORATING RITUALS, YOU CREATE MOMENTS OF CONNECTION, FOCUS AND MAGIC IN YOUR EVERYDAY LIFE.

ONE-POT SPICY GINGER STICKY TOFFEE PUDDING

A SUCCESS SPELL

This one-pot pud is delicious, dark and warming – but also promotes success and 'sticking' to your goals. Ginger was once one of the most prized and commonly traded spices in medieval England. It's well known for its healing properties, particularly for stomach issues, indigestion and bloating. Ginger warms the body and sooth aches and pains, and can sweat out fevers and colds. Innkeepers would even leave ginger at the bar for travellers to sprinkle into their beer to warm up. Unsurprising considering the powerful warming flavour profile, in folk magic ginger is associated with bringing energy and sparking action – it is most often used in money and success spells.

MOON PHASE: FULL MOON – **amplifies your goals and brings success to fruition.**

DAY OF THE WEEK: SUNDAY – **ruled by the Sun, symbolizing success and vitality.**

CANDLE COLOUR: YELLOW – **stimulates creativity and achievement.**

INCENSE: CINNAMON – **boosts energy and success.**

CRYSTAL: SUNSTONE – **encourages confidence and achievement.**

SERVES 1

FOR THE PUDDING:
1 tbsp chopped dates
2 tbsp chopped stem ginger in syrup
50ml (3½ tbsp) hot water (ideally moon water created under a full moon)
1 tbsp dark brown sugar
1 tbsp butter
2 tbsp spelt flour
½ tsp ground black pepper
1 tbsp rye flour
1 tsp baking powder
1 tbsp black strap molasses

FOR TOPPING:
1 tbsp butter
1 tbsp brown sugar
50ml (3 ½ tbsp) hot water
Flaked sea salt

Preheat the oven to 180°C/350°F/Gas 4. You'll need a ceramic baking dish that's a single-serving size for this no-mess one-pot recipe.

First, add your dates and ginger to the dish, along with the hot water, and stir. Let it sit for a few minutes, then add the rest of your pudding ingredients and mix. Top with the butter, sugar and water, but do not mix – just let them sit on the top of the batter. Sprinkle with a pinch of flaked salt and bake for 20 minutes in the preheated oven. As you savour the aroma of warmth and sweetness while the pudding cooks, write down one goal or thing that would aid you in sparking action toward your success. Once ready, the best way to enjoy this is with bare feet on the earth.

Concentrate on visualizing your goal, enjoying the potent properties of this gingery pud! Once finished, recite this incantation before closing the circle:

Ginger's fire, my intention written,
Swallowed whole, chewed and bitten.
A commitment made, to which I'll stick,
Bring it in, and bring it quick.

SAFFRON DAHL

A SPELL FOR BUSINESS SUCCESS OR A PAY RISE

Saffron, often considered the 'golden spice', is a symbol of wealth, success and abundance. It's believed to open pathways to new opportunities and bring good fortune into one's life. In India, saffron is associated with purity and vitality, often used in offerings and rituals to invoke blessings of prosperity. Lentils (the base of this dahl) are tied to endurance, patience and balance, all essential traits when striving for success. Together, saffron and lentils create a dish that aligns with powerful manifestations of career growth, stability and achievement.

MOON PHASE: WAXING MOON – supports growth and new ventures.

DAY OF THE WEEK: WEDNESDAY – ruled by Mercury, for communication and business success.

CANDLE COLOUR: GOLD OR GREEN – to attract wealth and recognition.

INCENSE: BERGAMOT – encourages luck and success.

CRYSTAL: TIGER'S EYE – promotes confidence and practical success.

SERVES 4

1 tbsp coconut oil
1 small onion, finely chopped
2 garlic cloves, minced
1 tsp ground turmeric
1 tsp ground cumin
1 tsp garam masala
200g (7oz) red lentils
750ml (3¼ cups) vegetable broth or water
A pinch of saffron threads
Juice of 1 lemon
Sea salt and black pepper
Fresh coriander (cilantro) and mint, chopped

Begin by lighting a green or gold candle, focusing on your intention for success and abundance in your life.

In a large pot, heat the coconut oil over medium heat. Sauté the onion until soft, then add the garlic and cook until fragrant. Stir in the turmeric, cumin and garam masala, allowing the spices to bloom and release their energy into the air. Add the red lentils and sauté for another 2 minutes. Gently pour in the vegetable broth, then add the saffron threads, stirring in the energy of the golden spice. As you stir, repeat the following:

Threads of saffron, fortune's weave,
Success I am destined to achieve.
Business blooms, my worth is shown,
Let my efforts now be known.

Let the dahl simmer for 25–30 minutes, until the lentils are tender and the dish is thick and creamy. Season with salt and pepper, then finish with a squeeze of fresh lemon juice for clarity. Sprinkle with freshly chopped coriander and mint before serving.

As you enjoy this nourishing dahl, reflect on your desires for success and the path ahead. Visualize your goals coming to fruition, allowing the dish to empower you in your journey.

CAROB BABKA

A PROSPERITY SPELL

Carob has a rich and fascinating history. Often called the 'chocolate of the ancient world', the seeds were used to weigh gold. This is where we derive the word 'carat' – making carob the perfect representation for prosperity in baking spells (as baking always signifies growth). In modernity, carob has been overshadowed by chocolate – although it is often used as a naturally caffeine-free substitute. Carob, however, has a unique honey-caramel flavour that outshines chocolate for sweetness. This ritual recipe can be used to conjure up prosperity of all kinds, but is particularly potent for those seeking wealth. As you knead, rise, bake and eat, infuse each step with your intention for prosperity and abundance.

MOON PHASE: WAXING MOON – for growing success and fortune.

DAY OF THE WEEK: THURSDAY– ruled by Jupiter, ideal for expanding opportunities.

CANDLE COLOUR: GOLD – represents prosperity and success.

INCENSE: FRANKINCENSE – uplifts and attracts abundance.

CRYSTAL: PYRITE – fosters ambition and financial prosperity.

SERVES 6–8

FOR THE DOUGH:
1 tsp instant dried yeast
1 tbsp sugar
60ml (¼ cup) warm water (ideally moon water created under a waxing moon)
300ml (1¼ cups) milk of your choice
90g (6 tbsp) butter
450g (3½ cups) plain (all-purpose) flour, plus extra for dusting
½ tsp sea salt

FOR THE FILLING:
50g (¼ cup) light brown sugar
4 tbsp carob powder
1 tsp ground cinnamon
60g (¼ cup) butter, softened
A pinch of sea salt

FOR THE SYRUP:
50g (¼ cup) caster (superfine) sugar

Combine the yeast, sugar and warm water in a bowl and set aside for 10 minutes to allow the yeast to activate – it'll be frothy and bubbly once it's ready.

Gently heat the milk and butter on the stove until the butter is melted. Leave to cool slightly, until warm.

Combine the flour and salt in a bowl. Add the yeast and milk mixtures. Stir everything together to form a shaggy dough, then tip it onto a floured work surface and knead for around 5–8 minutes, using extra flour where needed, until the dough is smooth and elastic. As you knead, visualize the prosperity you wish to manifest. Cover with a damp tea towel and prove for at least 1 hour, or until doubled in size. Meanwhile, grease and line a 900-g (2-lb) loaf pan.

To make the filling, beat the sugar, carob powder and cinnamon into the butter along with a pinch of salt. Make sure it is thoroughly combined.

Once your dough is proved, knock it back with a punch. Roll it out on a lightly floured surface with a rolling pin into a rectangular shape measuring roughly 35 x 25cm (14 x 10 inches) and spread your filling evenly over the dough. From a shorter end, roll the dough into a tight log, then cut in half lengthwise to expose the filling layers. With cut sides up, braid the two halves together to make a plait. As you braid the loaf, recite the following incantation:

As dough expands, prosperity grows,
Abundance flows where effort shows.
Twist and weave with mindful care,
Rituals, not habits, weave wealth to share.

RECIPE CONTINUES OVERLEAF

Place the babka into the prepared loaf pan, squishing it down if need be. Cover with a damp tea towel and leave to prove for 30 minutes more. Toward the end of the proving time, preheat the oven to 180°C/350°F/Gas 4.

Once proved, bake the babka for 45 minutes until golden on top.

While the babka is baking, make the syrup for glazing. Put the sugar in a saucepan with 60ml (¼ cup) water and gently heat until the sugar dissolves. Brush the glaze generously onto your babka straight out of the oven. Keep going until all the syrup is spent as you chant:

Maple sweet, prosperity neat,
Abundance be complete.

Leave to cool before slicing to serve.

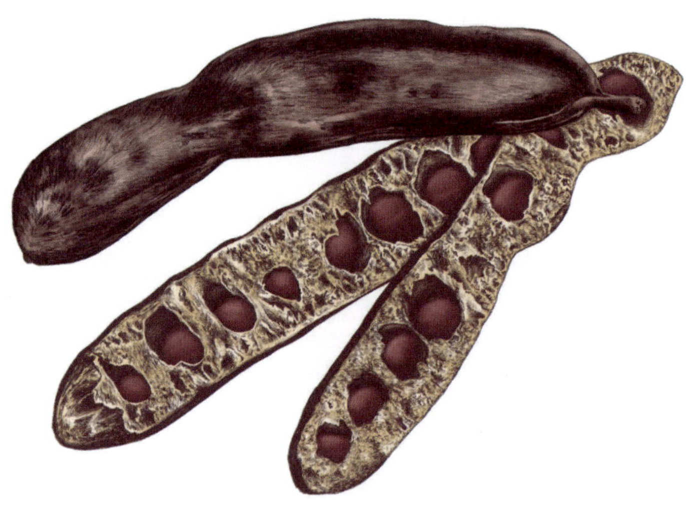

PEA AND MINT SOUP

A SPELL FOR PROTECTION FROM ILL INTENT

Peas have long held a place in folklore; they were used in sympathetic magic to ward off unwanted things, such as warts. Mint, with its fresh, clean scent, is known to offer protection from negative energy and ill wishes.

MOON PHASE: WANING MOON – banishes negativity and reinforces protection.

DAY OF THE WEEK: TUESDAY – ruled by Mars, for protective energy.

CANDLE COLOUR: BLACK – wards off harm and absorbs negativity.

INCENSE: MYRRH – creates a protective barrier.

CRYSTAL: BLACK TOURMALINE – shields against negativity.

SERVES 4

50g (3½ tbsp) butter
1 onion, finely chopped
1 leek, white part only, chopped
1 litre (4¼ cups) vegetable stock
750g (6 cups) frozen peas
2 tbsp chopped fresh mint, plus extra sprigs to garnish
Sea salt and black pepper

FOR THE SOUR CREAM:
4 tbsp sour cream
1 tbsp lemon juice
1 tbsp chopped fresh mint

Melt the butter in a large pot over medium heat, then add the chopped onion and leek. Cook gently for about 10 minutes, stirring occasionally, until the vegetables are softened but not browned.

Pour in the vegetable stock and bring the mixture to a simmer, allowing it to cook for around 15 minutes until the vegetables are tender. Add the frozen peas and continue cooking for another 5 minutes, just until the peas are tender and vibrant. Stir in the chopped mint, season with salt and pepper to taste, then remove the pot from the heat. Use a blender to blend the soup until smooth and creamy.

In a separate bowl, mix the sour cream with the lemon juice and chopped mint to create a tangy mint cream topping.

To serve, ladle the soup into bowls and carefully blob the mint cream on top, loosely forming the initials of the person or thing you seek protection from. Sprinkle a pinch of sea salt over the soup for added purification and recite the following before tucking in:

Green peas and mint, protect me now,
With every bite, I seal the vow.
Harm and worry, I cast away,
Shield me strong, come what may.

Stir the cream topping into the soup and enjoy. As you eat, visualize the protective energies of the peas and mint enveloping you, and symbolically destroy the harmful forces with each bite.

BEFORE MODERN MEDICINE, PEOPLE COMBINED MEDICINAL AND MAGICAL IDEAS TO DETERMINE PLANT USES. THE DOCTRINE OF SIGNATURES, A FOLK HERBALISM BELIEF, TAUGHT THAT 'LIKE TREATS LIKE', SO PLANTS RESEMBLING BODY PARTS COULD TREAT AILMENTS OF THOSE PARTS. FOR INSTANCE, EYEBRIGHT WAS USED FOR EYE PROBLEMS, AND NAMES LIKE 'LIVERWORT' AND 'KIDNEY BEANS' ALSO REFLECT THIS IDEA. THOUGH THE DOCTRINE'S EFFECTIVENESS WAS OFTEN QUESTIONABLE AND SOMETIMES HARMFUL, CERTAIN PLANTS DO BENEFIT THE BODY PARTS THEY RESEMBLE: WALNUTS SUPPORT BRAIN FUNCTION, TOMATOES AID HEART HEALTH, AND GRAPEFRUIT, WHICH RESEMBLES THE BREAST, HAS CANCER-FIGHTING PROPERTIES.

SALT-BURIED BAKED POTATOES WITH CRISPY SAGE BUTTER

A SPELL FOR GROUNDING AND PROTECTION

Salt has long held a prominent role in witchcraft and folk magic, renowned for its protective and purifying properties. In many cultures, salt is seen as a symbol of purity, used to cleanse spaces of negative energy, banish evil spirits and ward off malevolent forces. Historically, salt's value as a preservative – stopping decay – extended to spiritual beliefs, where it was thought to preserve the soul from corruption. In folklore, lines of salt at doorways or windowsills are said to prevent spirits or witches from entering a home. This belief has permeated pop culture; characters in movies and TV use salt circles for protection against demons and other supernatural beings. Similarly, in European traditions, spilling salt was considered bad luck, linked to betrayal and misfortune, as seen in Da Vinci's painting *The Last Supper*, where Judas is depicted knocking over a salt cellar. From ancient practices to modern media, salt remains a powerful symbol of defence against unseen forces. Sage, along with rosemary and garlic, is another plant that is integral to a witch's kitchen. Held in high regard due to its medicinal properties, sage, it's no surprise, is connected with wisdom and protection. As with rosemary, it is particularly potent for women, and is said to flourish in a household where women are in charge.

MOON PHASE: FULL MOON – **strengthens protective energies.**

DAY OF THE WEEK: SATURDAY – **ruled by Saturn, aligns with protection and stability.**

CANDLE COLOUR: WHITE – **symbolizes purity and protective light.**

INCENSE: SAGE – **purifies and protects the space.**

CRYSTAL: OBSIDIAN – **powerful for grounding and protection.**

SERVES 4 (AS A SIDE DISH)

500g (1lb 2oz) baby new potatoes
500g (1lb 2oz) sea salt
1 bulb of raw garlic
3 bay leaves
60g (¼ cup) unsalted butter, softened
2 tbsp finely chopped fresh sage
1 tbsp cracked black pepper

Preheat your oven to 200°C/400°F/Gas 6.

Carefully score your initials (or the initials of who you'd like to protect) into three of the potatoes. Put around one-third of your salt into the bottom of a skillet or sturdy baking pan. Lay your potatoes on top, and nestle the cloves of a garlic bulb and the bay leaves between them. Spray with some water – just enough to moisten. If you don't have a spray bottle, you can first rub the potatoes with salt and a little water and then transfer in your baking ban. Pour the remaining salt on top – use as much as you need to completely cover the potatoes – and bake for 35–40 minutes (until a fork can pierce the middle of one easily).

To prepare the sage butter, simply add a little of the butter to a pan and gently fry off your chopped sage for no more than a couple of minutes. Fold this into your remaining butter along with the cracked black pepper.

SAGE CAN EVEN PROTECT YOU FROM THE DENTIST; CHEWING SAGE LEAVES CUTS DOWN ON CAVITY FORMING BACTERIA IN THE MOUTH!

Once the potatoes are cooked, you get the enviable job of cracking the salt crust. As you break the seal, repeat the following incantation:

In salt and earth, buried deep,
Lies the essence of those who keep.
This charm's embrace, a shield of calm,
Protecting all from hurt and harm.

Once the salt is cracked, the spell is complete and the salt can be used again – but I suggest throwing at least a tablespoon into a body of water or into the earth to cast away the negativity.

Prise your potatoes from their salt crust and dust them off. The indentations left in the salt by the potatoes can even be used for divination – the method of divination with salt is called 'alomancy'. Dip the potatoes into the butter and enjoy, focusing on the protective qualities you have just invited in.

GARLIC WASN'T JUST USED TO PROTECT AGAINST VAMPIRES BUT ALSO WITCHES, DEMONS AND ILL WISHES. THIS FOLKLORE BEGAN IN ROMANIA, WHERE THE CLOVES WERE STUFFED INTO THE CORPSES OF SUSPECTED VAMPIRES TO KEEP LINGERING EVIL FORCES AT BAY.

GARLIC CLOVE AND OLIVE OIL LENTIL SOUP

A SPELL FOR PROTECTION FROM A WINTER COLD

Garlic is one of the most potent ingredients in any store cupboard, but particularly the witch's pantry. Folk have known for thousands of years that it has powerful health benefits, but many cultures have revered not just its medicinal properties but also its superstitious lore. Garlic is a protector above all else. The bulbs would be eaten before embarking on dangerous feats or journeys, evil spirits were thought to be averse to it, and ancient Greek midwives hung it in birthing rooms to keep evil forces away. For flavour, as an antiseptic and beyond, garlic wasn't just eaten to release its power – it was often worn or even buried as part of a ritual. We know today that garlic contains over 30 medicinal compounds – it's antiseptic, antiviral and even an aphrodisiac.

MOON PHASE: WANING MOON – to banish illness and strengthen defences.

DAY OF THE WEEK: MONDAY – ruled by the Moon, for healing and emotional balance.

CANDLE COLOUR: WHITE – promotes health and protection.

INCENSE: EUCALYPTUS – cleanses and wards off illness.

CRYSTAL: FLUORITE – supports immunity and energetic protection.

SERVES 4

3 bulbs of garlic
60ml (4 tbsp) olive oil
3 large shallots, chopped
1 tbsp soy sauce
2 tbsp tahini
900ml (3¾ cups) vegetable stock (depending how thick you like your soup)
3 bay leaves
¼ tsp of food-grade dragon's blood powder
200g (7oz) lentils
Juice of 3 lemons
Sea salt and black pepper
Crusty bread, to serve

Begin by creating a protective space in your kitchen. Light a white candle and place it near your cooking area.

Preheat the oven to 180°C/350°F/Gas 4. Place the whole garlic bulbs in a small dish and drizzle with 3 tablespoons of the olive oil. Cover with foil and roast for around 1 hour until caramelized.

In a large pot, heat the remaining olive oil and sauté the chopped shallots until softened. As you cook, drizzle in the soy sauce and season with salt and pepper. Stir in the tahini – it will coat your ingredients in a thick paste.

Next, add the vegetable stock, a bit at a time, stirring to loosen the tahini. Toss in the bay leaves (which are known for their protective properties) and stir in the dragon's blood powder (a powerful ingredient for banishing negativity). Finally, add the lentils and allow the soup to simmer for about 30 minutes until the lentils are soft. As it cooks, visualize your intentions for protection manifesting in the warm, bubbling soup.

Once the lentils are tender, remove your garlic from the oven. Set the garlic bulbs aside to cool slightly and immediately pour the hot garlic oil from the dish over the soup, watch it crackle and bubble. Once cool enough, use your fingers to squeeze the soft garlic flesh out of the skins into the soup. This is a satisfying task that tangibly represents imbuing the soup with the protective power of the garlic. As you squeeze the soft cloves in, repeat the following:

With these cloves of thirty-three aligned,
Garlic wards what chills may find.
Lentil broth and oil combine,
To build a wall both strong and kind.

Off the heat, add the lemon juice, stirring anticlockwise to amplify the protective properties of your dish.

Serve the soup in a cozy setting, enjoying it with crusty bread.

TAHINI BLONDIES

A SPELL TO REVEAL SECRETS!

'Open sesame!' Most of us, I am sure, are familiar with this phrase and its association with parlour magic and magicians. The saying comes from the Arabian Nights and refers to the opening of the sesame pod when the seeds are mature and ready. Sesame seeds have not only been a symbol of immortality in early Hindu legends, but in folk magic they are a tool for revealing hidden secrets and even treasures. You can use this recipe for focus when you need clarity on a decision, when you want information to be revealed to you, or if you have lost something important!

MOON PHASE: FULL MOON – illuminates hidden truths.

DAY OF THE WEEK: MONDAY – ruled by the Moon, for intuition and insight.

CANDLE COLOUR: PURPLE – enhances psychic awareness.

INCENSE: SANDALWOOD – encourages introspection and promotes focus.

CRYSTAL: LABRADORITE – uncovers hidden truths.

MAKES 9

200g (1 cup) brown sugar
160g (5¾oz) tahini
60ml (¼ cup) neutral oil (such as groundnut or sunflower)
60ml (¼ cup) milk of your choice
2 tsp vanilla extract or vanilla bean paste
170g (1¼ cups) plain (all-purpose) flour
½ tsp sea salt
½ tsp baking powder
4 tbsp sesame seeds, for sprinkling

Preheat the oven to 200°C/400°F/Gas 6 and grease or line a 20-cm (8-inch) square brownie pan.

To a mixing bowl, add your sugar, tahini and oil, and stir together into a paste. Mix in your milk and vanilla. Add the flour, salt and baking powder and mix. Transfer the dough to the prepared pan and spread into the corners. Bake for 15–20 minutes until slightly golden.

Once baked, sprinkle the sesame seeds on top and press them into the brownies (careful not to burn yourself – you may want to use a spoon or spatula for this). As you do so, repeat the following:

Stir and bake with magic's power,
The spell takes hold this very hour.
What was concealed, let us see,
Unlocked at last – open sesame!

Remove from the pan and leave to cool, then slice up and enjoy while focusing on what you want to be revealed!

IF THE CONCEPT OF USING PLANT POWER FOR TRANSFORMATION IS A NEW EXPERIMENT FOR YOU, IT'S BEST TO TEST OUT A WIDE VARIETY OF INGREDIENTS – AND ALWAYS WITH CAUTION IF A PLANT OR SUBSTANCE IS UNFAMILIAR. YOU WILL FIND THAT SOME OF THESE INGREDIENTS BECOME ONES THAT YOU USE AGAIN AND AGAIN, WHEREAS OTHERS SIMPLY WON'T BE FOR YOU. EVERYBODY IS DIFFERENT AND THERE IS NO ONE-SIZE-FITS-ALL. THE POINT OF KITCHEN MAGIC IS TO MAKE IT AS ADAPTABLE AS POSSIBLE SO THAT YOU CAN SEW CEREMONY AND INTENTION INTO YOUR LIFE IN THE SIMPLEST, MOST SATISFYING AND MOST DELICIOUS WAY POSSIBLE!

ORANGE AND BASIL RISOTTO

A SPELL FOR A NEW JOB

Orange is a powerful symbol of new beginnings, creativity and positive transformation. Basil, known for its ability to bring protection and success, is associated with overcoming obstacles and opening new doors. Together, these ingredients help nurture an environment where growth, clarity and prosperity can flourish. This orange and basil risotto, with its earthy undertones and fresh, vibrant flavours, represents the balance of creativity and courage needed to manifest new professional opportunities. As you cook, focus on your intention for success, whether it's a new job, promotion or career path.

MOON PHASE: WAXING MOON – **attracts opportunities.**

DAY OF THE WEEK: WEDNESDAY – **ruled by Mercury, for communication and professional success.**

CANDLE COLOUR: GREEN – **for growth and opportunity.**

INCENSE: PEPPERMINT – **clears obstacles and invites success.**

CRYSTAL: AVENTURINE – **promotes career advancement.**

SERVES 4

1 tbsp olive oil
1 small onion, finely chopped
2 garlic cloves, minced
1 tbsp chopped fresh basil, plus extra leaves to decorate
200g (heaped 1 cup) Arborio rice
100ml (scant ½ cup) white wine (optional)
750ml (3¼ cups) vegetable broth
Zest and juice of 1 large orange
100g (3½oz) cheese of your choice
Sea salt and black pepper

Begin by lighting the green candle and setting your intention to manifest success.

In a large saucepan, heat the olive oil over medium heat and sauté the onion until soft and translucent. Add the garlic and cook until fragrant, then stir in the fresh basil to infuse its protective energy. Add the rice and toast it lightly for 1–2 minutes.

Pour in the white wine (if using) and let it evaporate, then begin ladling in the vegetable broth, one spoonful at a time, stirring constantly. As the rice absorbs the broth, slowly add the zest and juice of the orange. Continue adding the broth, stirring over a gentle heat, until the rice is tender and creamy. Stir in the cheese for richness, then season with salt and pepper to taste.

Before serving, place a fresh basil sprig on top, as a final blessing for protection and success and recite:

Orange bright, basil bold,
A new opportunity soon unfolds.
Through this dish, my fate aligns,
A fresh new job, in perfect time.

While eating, reflect on your intentions and the journey ahead, and allow the energy of the dish to nurture your goals.

FENNEL SALT AND BLACK PEPPER SPRINKLE

A SPELL FOR WHEN YOU NEED SOMETHING – QUICKLY!

Fennel has a curious connection to 'quickness' – the town of Marathon is said to be named after fennel. Folklore has it that snakes would consume it before shedding their skin and it is therefore associated with renewal and transformation too. Interesting then that it has also always been used as a 'slimming' aid. Fennel has been a powerful digestive aid since ancient times – after Tudor feasts, sugared fennel seeds would be nibbled as a digestif – and it is also heralded as a cure for kidney stones and cystitis.

Fennel is a powerful tool for protecting one's home and possessions and was hung above doorways on midsummer's eve to keep evil spirits away. Like cumin, it is a 'keeper' which will help keep your home and possessions from being taken from you. It was stuffed into key holes to unlock this protective power. Fennel can be found growing wild all over, but it favours rocky cliffs. It is said to be better to forage than to grow ('sow fennel, sow trouble' so the saying goes), as growing it was thought to bring bad luck.

MOON PHASE: WAXING MOON – **boosts rapid manifestation.**

DAY OF THE WEEK: WEDNESDAY – **ruled by Mercury, speeds up intentions.**

CANDLE COLOUR: YELLOW – **for clarity and quick action.**

INCENSE: LEMONGRASS – **stimulates swift results.**

CRYSTAL: CLEAR QUARTZ – **amplifies intention.**

MAKES 500G (1lb 2oz)

100g (3½oz) wild fennel, chopped
100g (3½oz) black peppercorns
400g (14oz) coarse sea salt

Preheat the oven to 50°C/120°F/Gas 1 and line a baking tray with baking parchment.

Blend your fennel and peppercorns in a pestle and mortar until a paste is formed. Throw in your salt and mix until combined. Transfer to the prepared baking tray and bake for 15 minutes, then turn off the heat and allow it to cool inside the oven for around an hour.

Sprinkle a little of this mixture onto any dish (or recipe ritual) when you want to manifest potency, transformation and speed – each time you do so, repeat the following:

Sprinkle, sprinkle, swift and bright,
Hurry up, the time's just right!

MAGIC OFTEN WORKS IN WAYS WE CAN'T PREDICT. SOMETIMES, OUR WISHES ARE FULFILLED, BUT IN FORMS WE NEVER EXPECTED. THIS REMINDS US THAT WHILE WE MAY HAVE A VISION OF HOW THINGS SHOULD UNFOLD, THE UNIVERSE MAY HAVE OTHER PLANS. TRUST IN THE PROCESS, REMAIN OPEN-MINDED, AND RECOGNIZE THAT EVEN WHEN EVENTS DON'T MATCH OUR INITIAL DESIRES, THEY MIGHT LEAD TO SOMETHING EVEN BETTER THAN WE COULD HAVE IMAGINED. MAGIC WORKS IN MYSTERIOUS, UNEXPECTED WAYS – SOMETIMES, IT'S ALL ABOUT PERSPECTIVE!

SOUR CHERRY BALSAMIC BROWNIES

A TRANSFORMATION SPELL

The rich, tart flavour of these brownies comes from the balsamic glaze, made from grape must. In folklore, grapes symbolize abundance, fertility and prosperity. Associated with gods of wine and harvest like Dionysus and Bacchus, grapes embody joy, celebration and the cycle of life, as well as transformation, with their fermentation into wine seen as a magical process turning the simple into the divine. They also represent the balance between indulgence and temperance, embodying both life's sweetness and the need for moderation. This recipe is a reminder that you do not have to wait for a new year or a special day to make transformative changes. You can take action and change your path any time you choose to.

MOON PHASE: NEW MOON – **marks a fresh start and transformation.**

DAY OF THE WEEK: SUNDAY – **ruled by the Sun, for transformation and personal growth.**

CANDLE COLOUR: PURPLE – **symbolizes transformation and power.**

INCENSE: SANDALWOOD– **supports spiritual change.**

CRYSTAL: TIGER'S EYE – **aids in confidence, transformation and clarity.**

SERVES 2

240g dark (bittersweet) chocolate
90ml (6 tbsp) oil (groundnut or other)
250g (1¼ cups) light brown sugar
100ml (scant ½ cup) balsamic glaze
210g (1½ cups) plain (all-purpose) flour
50g (½ cup) cocoa powder
½ tsp sea salt
80g (2¾oz) dried sour cherries

IF YOU'D LIKE A BIGGER BROWNIE OR TO PERFORM THIS RITE AS PART OF A COVEN WITH THREE OTHERS, DOUBLE THE INGREDIENT QUANTITIES, USE A 30-CM (12-INCH) SQUARE TIN AND ADD 10 MINUTES TO THE COOKING TIME.

Preheat the oven to 160°C/320°F/Gas 3 and line a 20-cm (8-inch) square brownie pan with baking parchment.

Gently heat the chocolate and oil together in a saucepan until all the chocolate has melted. Add the sugar and balsamic glaze and stir in.

Combine all the remaining ingredients in a large bowl. Pour the chocolate mixture into the bowl and stir. Once combined into a batter, pour into the prepared pan and bake for 30 minutes.

As the brownies cook, write down 12 ways in which you would like to see your life or yourself be transformed. These can be big or small.

Let the brownies cool, but enjoy while still warm and a bit gooey for the most comforting effect. Cut the brownie into 12 bite-sized cubes to eat at midnight – each piece representing a desire you have to bring about a transformation into your life. Before eating each brownie bite, recite aloud the decree below. Feel free to also vocalize your personal intentions with each bite, but if performing this ritual in a group setting, you may prefer to keep them private.

With the first bite, I release the past,
The second bite clears my fears fast.
The third bite brings me to the now,
With the fourth, I make a powerful vow.
The fifth bite lets me shed all doubt,
The sixth bite casts all obstacles out.
The seventh bite welcomes in what's new,
The eighth bite brings vision, clear and true.
The ninth bite sheds all past shame,
The tenth bite ignites my inner flame.
The eleventh bite honours my self and soul,
The twelfth bite makes me fully whole.

THE WELCOME HOME VANILLA CHAI LOAF

A SPELL TO FIND A HOME, BUY A HOME OR KEEP A HAPPY HOME

This vanilla chai loaf is infused with warm, cozy spices, creating a welcoming atmosphere for a home or a space in need of comfort. Baking with intention, especially when working toward creating a happy home, can help manifest peace and prosperity. It's the reason I found my narrowboat home, and I bake this loaf once a year to keep my space sacred and filled with joy. As you prepare this cake, focus on your wishes for your home, symbolizing a safe, nurturing environment for all who dwell within it.

MOON PHASE: NEW MOON – sets intentions for new beginnings.

DAY OF THE WEEK: THURSDAY – ruled by Jupiter, for expansion and blessings.

CANDLE COLOUR: BROWN – connected to home, stability, and grounding.

INCENSE: CINNAMON – brings warmth and stability.

CRYSTAL: SMOKY QUARTZ – fosters grounding and home blessings.

MAKES 1 LOAF

190g (1½ cups minus 1 tbsp) plain (all-purpose) flour
150g (¾ cup) brown sugar
1 tbsp baking powder
1 tsp ground cinnamon (plus 1 tbsp for threshold magic)
½ tsp ground ginger
½ tsp ground cloves
½ tsp ground allspice
¼ tsp ground cardamom
¼ tsp ground nutmeg
180ml (¾ cup) milk
60ml (¼ cup) vegetable oil
2 tsp vanilla extract
2 tbsp maple syrup

YOU WILL ALSO NEED:
A small heatproof key
A piece of smoky quartz

Before you start, place the 1 tablespoon of cinnamon in your palm and blow it through the open threshold of your home for protection.

Preheat your oven to 180°C/350°F/Gas 4. Grease and line a 900-g (2-lb) loaf pan.

In a large bowl, whisk together the flour, sugar, baking powder and ground spices. In a separate bowl, combine the milk, oil, vanilla extract and syrup. Pour the wet ingredients into the dry, mixing until smooth.

Carefully place a small, heatproof key (cleaned and wrapped in baking parchment) into the batter before pouring it into the loaf pan. Bake for 45–50 minutes, or until a skewer inserted into the centre of the loaf comes out clean.

After cooking, carefully slice and enjoy the loaf, being mindful not to bite the key! Repeat the following when you find and unwrap it:

In this loaf, baked with cheer,
A key inside, has now appeared.
Find my home or keep it bright,
May love and peace fill every night.

Once the loaf is finished and the key found, place the key and quartz somewhere prominent in your home, where you will see it every day, to serve as a reminder of your intentions.

CLOSING REMARKS

AS WE REACH THE END OF THIS JOURNEY TOGETHER, I WANT TO TAKE A MOMENT TO REFLECT. IT HAS BEEN AN INCREDIBLE HONOUR TO SHARE WITH YOU THE MAGIC THAT CAN BE FOUND IN EVERYDAY COOKING, AND THE POWERFUL CONNECTION WE CAN FORM WITH THE FOOD WE CREATE. MY HOPE IS THAT, THROUGH THIS BOOK, YOU'VE GAINED NOT ONLY PRACTICAL RECIPES BUT ALSO A DEEPER SENSE OF HOW FOOD CAN BECOME A BRIDGE TO SOMETHING MORE – SOMETHING TRANSFORMATIVE, SACRED AND PERSONAL.

The recipes and rituals we've explored here are meant to be starting points. They hold the foundational knowledge that will allow you to continue your own journey into kitchen witchery. Just as I have, I encourage you to experiment – trust your intuition and be open to the flow of inspiration that comes from both the ingredients themselves and the environment around you. These are not just recipes for sustenance; they are pathways to mindfulness, intention and self-discovery.

Food has always had the power to nurture, heal and sustain us physically, but it also holds the potential to guide us emotionally and spiritually. Through the intentional practice of kitchen magic, you've learned how to transform ordinary cooking into a meaningful ritual – one that brings not just nourishment but clarity, focus and balance to your life.

As you begin to craft your own recipes and rituals, I encourage you to remain open to the endless possibilities the seasons, ingredients and your own creativity can bring. Stay curious, continue learning and above all, stay safe in your magical practice. Always respect the properties and energies of the plants and ingredients you use, and never stop seeking the wisdom they offer. Just as the Wheel of the Year continues to turn, so too will your knowledge and experience deepen with time.

I want to thank you for walking this path with me. It has been a journey of sharing my heart and soul through these pages, and I hope that in some small way, I have been able to inspire and empower you to embrace the magic in your own life. Every time you stir a pot, bake bread, or brew a cup of tea with intention, you are weaving your own story into the fabric of the universe.

Remember, magic is not something far away or difficult to grasp. It lives in the ordinary moments – in the quiet stirrings of a wooden spoon, the fragrant herbs you sprinkle on a dish, and the warmth of a home-cooked meal shared with loved ones. The magic is always there, waiting for you to notice, to invite it in, and to make it a part of your life.

In parting, I leave you with this thought: cooking is an act of love, not just for those you cook for, but for yourself as well. With each meal, you have the opportunity to honour your body, your spirit and the earth that provides you with sustenance. Approach your kitchen with gratitude, with respect, and with a sense of wonder – through this shift, the magic will always find you.

May your kitchen always be filled with warmth, your meals with love, and your life with magic. Until we meet again, I wish you the brightest of blessings.

LAURA MAY

USEFUL REFERENCES AND STOCKISTS

Every effort has been made to ensure that the recipes in this book are accessible, often using dried ingredients as alternatives to fresh ones. I want everyone to experience the benefits of powerful plants and ingredients – not just those with access to fresh, foraged counterparts or the expertise to forage confidently. While I encourage foraging as a way to connect with nature and the land around you, I understand it's not feasible for everyone. These stockists provide an excellent alternative where foraging isn't possible.

STOCKISTS

STAR CHILD

Based in Glastonbury and one of my favourite bricks and mortar shops, Star Child offers a selection of dried herbs, resins and foraged ingredients. They ship within the UK, and international shipping is available on request.
Website: www.starchild.co.uk

JUSTINGREDIENTS

Supplies culinary and botanical dried herbs, including organic options, with international shipping available.
Website: www.justingredients.co.uk

WOODLAND HERBS

Provides herbal teas and botanicals, primarily shipping within the UK. For international orders, enquiries are recommended.
Website: www.woodlandherbs.co.uk

STARWEST BOTANICALS

Offers organic herbs, teas and spices with worldwide shipping available.
Website: www.starwest-botanicals.com

MOUNTAIN ROSE HERBS

Supplies organic and wildcrafted herbs, spices and foraged goods, with international shipping supported.
Website: www.mountainroseherbs.com

BULK HERB STORE

Provides a range of dried herbs and teas and ships to select international destinations.
Website: www.bulkherbstore.com

For any of these suppliers, check their shipping policies directly to ensure availability for your specific location.

FURTHER READING

FOOD FOR FREE BY RICHARD MABEY

A classic guide to foraging in the UK, offering practical advice and illustrations to help identify edible plants.

EDIBLE WILD PLANTS: WILD FOODS FROM DIRT TO PLATE BY JOHN KALLAS

A comprehensive guide to identifying and preparing wild edible plants in North America, suitable for beginners and experienced foragers.

CUNNINGHAM'S ENCYCLOPAEDIA OF MAGICAL HERBS BY SCOTT CUNNINGHAM

A foundational text for understanding the magical and folkloric uses of plants. Highly accessible for beginners in plant-based magic and herbalism. I use this book daily.

THE GREEN WITCH: YOUR COMPLETE GUIDE TO THE NATURAL MAGIC OF HERBS, FLOWERS, ESSENTIAL OILS, AND MORE BY ARIN MURPHY-HISCOCK

A practical guide blending plant-based witchcraft with holistic living.

THE HANDMADE APOTHECARY: HEALING HERBAL REMEDIES BY VICKY CHOWN AND KIM WALKER

A practical guide to crafting natural remedies with plants, blending foraging with herbal medicine.

BRAIDING SWEETGRASS: INDIGENOUS WISDOM, SCIENTIFIC KNOWLEDGE, AND THE TEACHINGS OF PLANTS BY ROBIN WALL KIMMERER

A poetic and thought-provoking exploration of our relationship with plants and nature, written by a botanist with a deep respect for indigenous traditions.

These books provide a mix of practical foraging knowledge and insight into the rich folklore and magical traditions associated with plants.

INDEX

LAURA MAY

is a kitchen witch and content creator on
@lauramayritualkitchen (Instagram)
@theritualkitchen (TikTok)
and @Theritualkitchen (YouTube).
From her narrowboat, Laura shares
food spells and advice on modern witchcraft.